You Fill Up My Senses

(The Joy and Despair of Following Sheffield United)

By

Alan Allsop

Dedicated to all my fellow generation of Blades who have, over the years, seen defeat dragged out of the jaws of victory far too often to ever dare to presume we will triumph, yet they still turn out week after week in the hope that every once in a while our pessimistic views will be proven unfounded.

Acknowledgements

While this book is based on my memories of watching the Blades and the range of emotions, opinions, experiences and anecdotes come from the vast library of 'stuff' lodged in my head, I could not possibly have retained all of the many little details required to ensure that the story remains historically correct.

I would therefore like to thank the following for providing the resources necessary to put the whole thing together.

John Garrett, Sheffield United Supporter Liaison Officer/Club Historian, for pointing me in the right direction.

Denis Clarebrough and Andrew Kirkham for meticulously recording statistics in various books without which I would have been far less confident in recalling many of the dates, results and players mentioned.

Worldfootball.net for a variety of player statistics.

Stats.football.co.uk for league position snapshots.

Englishfootballleaguetables.co.uk for final tables and average attendance figures.

Transfermarkt.co.uk for details of player movements.

Wikipedia for a plethora of little details.

Skysports.com for some more recent stats.

YouTube channels: SUFC History, TJS Sports, Ziggazigahh, BladesUnitedCoUk, cestrian81, Robert Wolf, SUFC147, for video reminders of days gone by.

The Sheffield Star, The Yorkshire Post, The Daily Mail and The Independent for various articles of reference.

To Sheffield United FC, its players, staff and supporters for providing me with over fifty years of joy, despair, fun, frustration, laughter, tears and most of all a sense of belonging that has been the one constant in an otherwise ever changing lifetime.

And of course to my Dad, who passed away during the writing of this book, for getting me hooked in the first place.

While I am confident that the facts and figures contained within this book are correct to the best of my knowledge, that knowledge is reliant on information gathered from a variety of sources and while most details have been checked across at least two different sources I am unable to make absolute guarantees of their accuracy. It should also go without saying that any opinions given during the course of this story are solely those of the author.

Contents

Introduction

Following a football club is not about embarking on a trail of glory. It is not about trophies, titles or any sustained level of success. If that is what it was all about then everyone would follow one of the so called '*Top Six*' clubs and every other club would fall by the wayside. Don't get me wrong, those big clubs do have a hard-core of loyal, lifelong fans and I tip my hat to them, but for every true fan of the 'big' clubs there are a number of hangers on and glory hunters claiming to be fans that would be off like a shot if the good times came to an end.

A true fan follows their club through thick and thin, and for most true fans it is usually thin. There are only so many prizes to win and there are far more teams than prizes so most clubs end up winning nothing year after year, yet we keep going, we keep the faith and every once in a while our team rewards us with a little piece of gold sifted out from the tons of gravel at the bottom of the stream that is league football.

We all choose our clubs for our own reasons. For some it is a family tradition (or to rebel against it.) For others it may be about where we are from. The reasons for choosing are many and varied, but, glory hunters aside, once chosen we tend to stick to our choices with the kind of loyalty and devotion that if mirrored in marriage would see divorce lawyers destitute.

I chose Sheffield United. I have never wavered or strayed and I never will. I don't profess to know about every other club, but I do know that following Sheffield United is about more than just football. Sheffield itself is a city like no other. It was forged in steel and the people of Sheffield reflect that. In the main Sheffielders are straight talking, hardworking, honest and slightly cynical folk who call a spade a spade and are fiercely proud of their traditions. United as a club, probably more so than our nearest neighbours, reflects these qualities within its own unique identity.

There is a subtle difference between the mind-sets of supporters of the clubs from Sheffield 2 (United) and Sheffield 6. While sharing the same sort of background and upbringing, fans of our neighbours will tend to see three straight wins as a sign that success is just around the corner while, with the same results, we will be quoting the law of averages and predicting a slip up on the horizon. Given the same short run of decent results, they see daffodils poking their heads through the deepest of snow while we see storm clouds gathering at the end of a hot summer's day. The other lot are mainly optimists who expect success to be just around the corner, and are therefore constantly disappointed, while we Blades are generally pessimists who expect to fall at the next hurdle and so, on the few occasions we succeed we are both surprised and delighted. Which would you rather be?

So why is this? Why do such loyal and devoted fans seem to have such low expectations of a club they clearly love?....Read on.

If Sheffield United were a dog it would not be a pedigree champion marching out at Crufts. It would not constantly win rosettes and trophies and draw appreciative stares from other dog owners. It would be a scruffy mongrel that shakes the muddy water off its coat all over your brand new trousers. It would eat the food off your plate while you step away to take a phone call. It would be the dog that that shits on the living room carpet when the door out to the garden is wide open. You know it will show you up when the most people are watching, you know it will let you down when you least expect it, you know it will sit quietly while the burglars steal everything you own, but every now and then it will offer you its paw to be shaken or actually bring back the stick that you have thrown for it and you will love it more than you could any fancy pampered poodle. You would not swap it for anything and you would do anything for it.

Just like that dog, it is the flaws and the frailties that make my club so special to me. It is the despair following the relegations and humiliating defeats that make the promotions, cup runs and unexpected victories so much more memorable and rewarding. Without those lows the highs would not be so special. That is why we all keep going; that is why we love them so much, that is being a Blade and this is the story of how I have seen the frustration and the elation over a lifetime of following my team.

The Early Seasons
1960-1970

My dad was a Blade and two of my uncles on my mother's side were Blades. Another uncle wore blue and white, which was sad, but at least it led to lively conversations at the weekends when the family would gather at my grandma's house on Page Hall Road.

I was born in 1960 when the Blades were in the Second Division, or what is now called The Championship. In the first season after my birth United finished in second place and were promoted to the top flight with Derek (Doc) Pace ending up top scorer with twenty six goals. They also reached the semi-finals of the FA Cup losing to Leicester City in a second replay after two 0-0 draws. I am oblivious to any of this as, being an infant; I was still struggling with keeping my food down and could regularly be found bawling my eyes out demanding the next nappy change.

The following season the Blades finished a creditable fifth place and also reached the quarter finals of both major cup competitions, so the 1962/63 season was something everyone was looking forward to, but ended in a mid-table tenth place finish. This was followed in the 1963/4 season by another mid-table finish as United ended the season in twelfth place, but at least seemed to have consolidated themselves in the top division. Again these are just historical facts. I could walk and talk by then, but the offside rule was still going way over my head.

At the start of the 1964/5 season my dad decided I was old enough to take my first trip to 'Beautiful Down Town Bramall Lane' and took me to see the Blades face Stoke City in the first home game of the season. Now I don't know if it was because of me being there, but we managed to lose the game one-nil and a mediocre season saw us finish in nineteenth place which was too close to the relegation zone for comfort.

In all honesty I have only vague recollections of attending that first game or the other games my dad took me to over the next couple of seasons, I know I went because I was told that I went and what few memories I have are more of being surrounded by lots of shouting men rather than of any particularly eventful games of football.

What I do remember from my visits to Bramall Lane over those first few seasons was picking up on the chanting of the crowd, in particular the chant of '*M.I.- M.I.C -M.I.C.K. Mick Jones*' aimed at our star striker who, almost as soon as I had discovered was one of Sheffield United's best players, was sold to Leeds United becoming the first of many stars of my generation to be snatched from the Blades by the evil, white shirted, talent thieves from Elland Road. Despite being relegated at the end of the 1967/68 season I was still taken to the odd few games each season and it is probably the fact that we were in the second tier, and therefore had something realistic to aim for, that that kept my attention and ultimately got me hooked for life.

1970/71

After a couple of so-so seasons in Division Two the 1970/71 season was the one that really got me hooked. I was getting older, being ten years old at the start of the season, and having started playing the game myself I was now watching the Blades with much more interest in what was happening on the pitch. In those so-so seasons the games were more memorable as being pretty rare days out with my dad and an introduction to crowds in far bigger numbers than I had been used to anywhere else as a child. My memories of those couple of seasons are more of listening to the songs that the throngs of rowdy youths stood at the back of the kop were singing. Bow legged chickens and knock kneed hens (ask any Blade over fifty five if you don't understand) spring to mind more than any results or performances. There seemed to be a wider variety of songs in those days, although quite a few of them referred to the skinhead culture that was around at that time and verses about swinging chains on Shoreham Street and kicking coppers in the bollocks were probably not what my dad really wanted me to hear. This season though I was actually watching the games and taking a real interest in what was going on.

I was still quite small, but managed to get a great view of the games standing behind the white wall towards the back corner of the Shoreham Street kop where many youngsters first stood to watch the Blades. There was a big drop below the wall and so the taller adults did not spoil the view. As well as the game I would

12

also watch as the crowd would sway all the way down the kop at each United attack and go wild when we scored a goal and I looked forward to the days when I would be big enough to join in with the rough and tumble behind the net.

The first home match of that magnificent season was against Swindon Town and United managed to beat them 2-1. I had been on holiday at Butlins the previous week and my dad had made sure we got back home on the Saturday in time to go to the Lane for the match while my mum unpacked the suitcase. I soon became familiar with the names of the United players, with Len Badger, Ted Hemsley, John Flynn, Billy Dearden, Geoff Salmons, Alan Woodward and of course Tony Currie becoming very familiar over the course of the season, although if asked I would have struggled to come up with the correct spelling for Eddie Colquhoun in those days.

I did not go to all of the home games back then as my dad regularly worked on Saturdays and was not always home in time to go to the match, but he took me when he could. The next time he took me I had my scarf nicked by a Leeds hooligan who, ever so bravely, picked on the ten year old me rather than take his chances with someone his own size after I had gone to the toilet during the game. I wasn't happy about that, but I was more pleased at the end of the game after a second half goal from Tony Currie knocked the Leeds bullies out of the League Cup.

The next game I went to was a special one, we were at home in the local derby against our cross city rivals and we managed to beat them 3-2 which, even then, I realised was something special to our fans. We had had some mixed results so far in the season, but this victory put us in sixth place and only four points behind leaders Leicester City. The results were mixed all season, but a 2-1 win over leaders Leicester on Boxing Day gave us hope that we might have a chance of promotion.

Manager John Harris re-jigged the team in January as John Tudor went to Newcastle with John Hope and David Ford coming the other way. At the same time the acquisition of the terrier like Trevor Hockey from Birmingham proved to be a master stroke as Hockey was given one simple instruction. 'Win the ball and give it to Tony Currie.' Which he did game after game and Currie did the rest.

13

As Easter came around a no score draw away to leaders Leicester set us up for the return match with our city rivals and I can remember standing at the front of their kop in a crowd of over forty seven thousand watching another 0-0 away draw. The game itself did not stick in my memory, but one thing I do remember was a copper getting his hat knocked off when someone threw an apple at him. After that game we were left in third position, but I remember my dad saying that we would struggle to catch Cardiff City as they had a game in hand and a better goal average. The pessimism seemed to be engrained even then.

Two home wins followed and when we managed to pick up a point away to Middlesbrough we were in the second promotion place with just two games to go. Even then my dad pointed out that Cardiff, who were just behind us still had a game in hand.

The next game was actually against Cardiff at Bramall Lane on a Tuesday night and my dad took me and my mate Brian Roberts to the match. They still had that game in hand over us so it was vital that we beat them and beat them we did. The game finished 5-1 to the Blades and I can remember me and Brian shouting '*We want six*,' with the rest of the crowd in the final minutes of the game. We had also improved our goal average (A confusing system that seemed to favour solid defending rather than open attacking play) so Cardiff would have to win their last two games by big margins and we would have to lose our last game, at home to Watford, if they were to be promoted instead of us. Even my dad had to concede that things looked good.

The following Saturday we confirmed our promotion to the First Division by totally outclassing Watford 3-0 at Bramall Lane and I was well and truly hooked. The team, consisting of *John Hope, Len Badger, Ted Hemsley, John Flynn, Eddie Colquhoun, Trevor Hockey, Alan Woodward, Geoff Salmons, Billy Dearden, Tony Currie and Gil Reece* played some brilliant football that day and it wasn't a game, but more an exhibition of quality football as we took Watford apart and cemented our return to the top tier. My first proper season watching the Blades had turned out to be one of the best ever and I couldn't wait to see them playing in the First Division the following season. Little did I know at that point that I was merely being lured into a false sense of security.

1971/72

The 1971/2 season could not have got off to a better start and with eight wins and two draws from our first ten games we sat proudly at the top of the league, three points clear of Manchester United. Stewart Scullion, who had impressed in the Watford side that were beaten as we gained promotion, had been added to the squad, but it was basically the team that had taken us up that led the assault on the top division. The highlight of the early season for me was going to Nottingham Forest where we won 3-2, the memory though was not particularly for the football or the result, but because a couple of weeks later the faces of me, my dad and my uncle were seen on the cover of a magazine called Football League Review. We had been unknowingly snapped as we watched the game from the terrace at the City Ground.

Our good start however was not to be maintained and after losing 2-0 at Old Trafford to a great Manchester United side, with their second goal being the one that always seems to be shown whenever George Best is mentioned on television, we began to struggle a little. Three more defeats, 3-2 to Stoke at home, 3-2 at Southampton and 2-1 at Manchester City followed by a 1-1 draw at home to Liverpool, where Currie hit a magnificent goal, saw us drop down the table and the reality of being back in the big time started to take hold. In that Liverpool game I also learnt, from the chanting of the crowd that, apparently, the Liverpool supporters live in slums and eat dead rats out of dustbins. It is surprising what you can find out at a football match.

With two points for a win in those days the league positions changed regularly and successive wins firstly away at West Ham and then at home to Coventry saw us climb back into joint second position on points before a 3-0 defeat at Derby dropped us back into fifth place. Nevertheless we were sat amongst esteemed company and the next game will be etched in my memory till the day I die.

My dad was unable to make all of the games and so I had been allowed to go to the odd match on the bus with friends. On the 27th of November 1971 I donned my fishtail parka and called for my mate Graham Green who lived on the Pye Bank estate in Sheffield. We walked into Sheffield city centre and onwards to Bramall Lane and got into the ground quite early. In those days there was usually some sort of pre-match entertainment laid on and we saw regular visits from a dog display team, which I think may have belonged to the RAF, or other times there would be some girl dancing troops on the pitch. Whatever entertainment was on it gave the early visitors to the ground something to keep them interested prior to the game.

Also in those days you could walk from the kop around to the Bramall Lane end by going around the cricket pitch and passing in front of the pavilion, so you could stand behind the goal United were attacking (rowdy away fans permitting) in both halves. This is just what Graham and I did, so we had the pleasure of standing behind the goal for each and every one of the seven goals that the Blades put past Ipswich Town that day. The team for that match was the same team that had seen us promoted against Watford the previous year. *John Hope, Len Badger, Ted Hemsley, John Flynn, Eddie Colquhoun, Trevor Hockey, Alan Woodward, Geoff Salmons, Billy Dearden, Tony Currie and Gil Reece.* Alan Woodward scored four of the goals (1 penalty) and the others came from Gil Reece, Len Badger and Billy Dearden. We caught the bus home and a bloke on the bus asked us the score and would not believe us when we said we had won 7-0.

The win lifted us back into third place with the likes of Leeds, Liverpool, Tottenham and Arsenal looking up at us. United however were not going to let us celebrate for too long and managed to lose the very next game 5-1 away to bottom club Crystal Palace. I did not go to that game, but I can clearly remember playing football on a muddy pitch on Wincobank Hill on that Saturday afternoon, and speculating how many the Blades were going to get, before returning home to be told we had been hammered by the Londoners. This was an early reminder to me that following the Blades was always going to be a rocky ride.

Two wins and three draws in the next five games saw us going into the third week in January in fifth place and still in touch with the leaders Manchester United, but things were about to take a turn for the worse. After losing 1-0 to Don Revie's Leeds United at Elland Road, a game I remember more for having to dodge hordes of Leeds hooligans as me and my uncle dashed to get back to his car after the game, we played Arsenal at home and were taken to the cleaners by the previous season's double winners. We lost 5-0

16

and never really recovered with just two wins coming in the next thirteen games. One of these games was a 0-0 draw at struggling Huddersfield Town where my abiding memory was of standing at the front of the side terracing and watching Alan Woodward's head bobbing along at the other side of the pitch. There was such a hump in the pitch that, from where I stood, the player's heads were all that you could see when the ball was at the opposite side of the ground. That poor run also included a 4-0 home defeat to eventual champions Derby County and saw us drop down the table before we rounded off the season with consecutive wins against Palace at home and Wolves away which saw us end the season in what I suppose, for a first season back up there, was a creditable tenth position, but it still felt disappointing after the brilliant start that we had made. Manchester United whose team included George Best, Bobby Charlton, Denis Law, Brian Kidd etc. had also slipped away, finishing just two points and two places ahead of us after an equally good start so I suppose we were in good company.

1972/73

The 1972/3 season started slowly in comparison to the previous year, but, after being thumped 5-0 away to Liverpool, successive 1-0 home victories over Manchester United and Arsenal saw us in a comfortable mid-table position after twelve games. Then typical of the Blades we managed only two wins and two draws in the next twelve games leaving us perilously close to the drop zone. Our squad size had increased over the last two seasons with Keith Eddy probably being the best of the additions, taking over from Trevor Hockey in the second half of the season, but while players like Jimmy Bone, Steve Faulkner, Steve Goulding and Alan Ogden raised the numbers I am not sure any of them added to the quality of the squad. A mixed bag of results saw us going into the last three games of the season comfortably clear of danger and a 2-1 away win at Manchester United followed by a point from a 1-1 draw at Ipswich and a final day 3-2 home win over Tottenham saw us finish the season in a solid twelfth place sandwiched between Manchester City and Chelsea. Oh to be sat between those two teams today!

While we had finished in a similar position to the previous season the route we had taken to get there was completely different and watching the Blades during that campaign had been far less exciting, but to me plucking the good results out of an indifferent run seemed to give as much, if not more pleasure than when we were winning regularly over the previous two years. 'Strength Through Adversity' as the saying in the Bramall Lane tunnel goes.

1973/74

The 1973/74 season set off with us fans expecting more of the same with a mid-table finish expected and we were to be neither disappointed nor surprised. With Keith Eddy now pulling the strings there was a little more guile in the defensive midfield position, but at times I thought we missed Hockey's tenacity. There were however some highlights along the way. The first of these was a 5-0 victory over Arsenal at Bramall Lane where Tony Currie delighted the crowd by sitting on the ball as he faced up to Alan Ball. The ginger international had done the same to Currie a couple of seasons earlier and now TC paid back the favour in style. Bad injuries to Eddy (broken collar bone) and keeper McAllister (broken leg) did not help things as we struggled to get results through the autumn.

In December of 1973 United changed their manager and John Harris, who had built what I consider to be the best ever United team I have seen, was replaced by Ken Furphy. This was the catalyst for my dad to stop going to the games and while he always retained an interest in the results he never went to Bramall Lane again. Furphy's reign started with similar results and performances to Harris and another great memory of this season was in a home game against Southampton. Currie, who was renowned for his ability to place a pass on a sixpence (old currency coin for younger readers) took a corner and placed the ball perfectly to Alan Woodward just outside the 'D' on the edge of the box. Woodward pivoted on his left leg and hammered a ferocious, unstoppable volley into the net in front of the Shoreham Street kop. The Blades won 4-2 and this game was followed by a 2-1 away victory at a now struggling Manchester United on Boxing Day.

Continuing mixed results going into 1974 and a real struggle to score goals in the second half of the season (Fourteen compared with thirty in the first half) saw us finish in thirteenth position, but, in a season where an aging Manchester United team were relegated, I suppose this was not such a bad result.

18

1974/75

Furphy led the Blades into the 1974/5 season with expectations higher as the new South Stand started to rise from the site of the former cricket pitch. Bramall Lane had always been a strange ground with three sides dedicated to the football terraces and the fourth side being the site of the cricket pitch and associated pavilion. People would actually sit in the cricket pavilion to watch games with the nearest touchline being a good hundred yards away. The view must have been terrible, even more so on the occasions when the television crews came and a scaffold was erected by the halfway line to hold the cameras. Now though, after believing we had established ourselves as a top tier club we were finally to have a proper four sided ground and the concrete structure grew as the season went on.

I was by now in my third year at comprehensive school and football was the big topic, amongst the boys anyway, and I would meet up with my mates to go to the home games, moving ever closer to the areas where the older lads would be singing and swaying down the kop. The songs were still many and varied and whilst most seemed to be aimed at the away supporters and the fate that awaited them outside, '*Over there, over there, and do they smell; like fucking hell,*'- '*You're going to get your fucking heads kicked in,*'-'*We'll see you all outside,*' and '*You're going home in a Sheffield ambulance.*' There were others that were slightly less threatening and maybe a little random, such as '*Mrs Hall's sausage rolls are the best, Mrs Hall's sausage rolls are the greatest, with the strawberry milk from her breast, and her husband does the rest; Na na na na na na na na na*' etc. I never could work that one out but it certainly got the younger fans swaying down the kop as the atmosphere built up.

It was a great time and we would return to school after a match and relay our stories to those who were still not allowed to go to the games. Away games were however still mainly attended with my uncle who had continued to take me around the country after my dad had stopped going to the games. On the odd occasion during this season, when my uncle could not make the games, I was allowed to go on the coach or the football special trains that were laid on at the time, but my parents were understandably reluctant to let me go to a lot of away games on my own as there was quite a problem with hooligans at the time. It was this social side of following a football team as well as the results of the Blades that made following them such an entertaining pastime and being able to turn up, pay on the gate, meet friends and stand together as a group is something that is sadly missing in todays all seater, all ticket environment.

Despite having sold one of our best players in Geoff Salmons there were still seven of the promotion winning team in the squad and newer faces like David Bradford, Colin Franks and Tony Field looked like giving us a bit of depth and balance and with Scottish goalkeeper Jim Brown now established as owner of the number one jersey we were still expecting decent things from the Blades as we looked forward eagerly to the new season.

The season itself turned out to be even better than most fans expected. After an indifferent start with two draws and a defeat the Blades strung together four successive wins. This run included a 3-1 victory over Ipswich Town, where Tony Field carried the ball past most of the Ipswich team to score a brilliant individual goal, as the Blades lifted themselves up the table. A run of mixed results then saw us drop down the league and after a Boxing Day defeat, 1-0 at Middlesbrough we were left in what was becoming our customary mid-table position.

Six matches unbeaten followed and in mid-February we were looking much stronger. A good March which included a famous game against West Ham at Bramall Lane where the Blades came from behind to win 3-2 with Tony Currie scoring what was described on TV as '*A quality goal from a quality player,*' saw us consolidate our position and keep within striking distance of the top clubs.

An unbeaten April including a 3-2 win at Everton, where I got ragged by a group of angry scousers who came around to confront the Blades fans on the side terrace after the third goal, and a 4-0 home victory over Leicester saw us going into the last game of the season with a good chance of qualifying for Europe.

The game was against Birmingham City at St Andrews and my uncle took me there in his company car. We collected our tickets for the match when we arrived at the ground and rather than being stood on the terraces I found myself sat in the main stand opposite the giant standing area where the Birmingham fans gathered.

Unlike at most other grounds the more rowdy Birmingham faithful stood on the terracing at the side of the pitch rather than behind the goal and on this night half of that side of the ground was taken up by thousands of Blades fans hoping for glory and a venture into Europe the following season. I was happy to be on the other side of the ground that night as there was sporadic fighting between the fans throughout the game which ended in a 0-0 draw. Towards the end of the game Tony Currie had a chance, but his shot from just outside the box went agonisingly over the bar and with that miss went our chances of European football the following season.

Outside the ground after the game The Birmingham hooligans were looking for blood and I was approached by a couple of them trying to spot anyone with a Yorkshire Accent. *'Have you got the time?'* said one of the Brummies, and I saved myself a good kicking by putting on my best Birmingham accent and saying *'No Sorry'* in the local dopey drawl.

The season had ended with the disappointment of missing out on Europe, but a sixth place spot just four points behind champions Derby County (who we lost to home and away) was still a good result and we were all left wondering what could have been. If those results against the Rams had been reversed, who knows, we could have been champions ourselves.

It seems strange now, looking back after all these years, that the highest finishing position I have ever seen in my lifetime of watching Sheffield United was greeted on that night by disappointment rather than elation, but that's football for you.

Despite the disappointment of missing out on Europe I was still proud of the Blades performance and the improvement in their finishing position and I went into the summer naively full of optimism for things to come the next season. Who knows, a four point improvement on this season and we could indeed be champions next year. With our England international Tony Currie pulling the strings anything was possible, wasn't it?

1975/76

1975 saw the opening of the new South Stand and the closing of an era of relative success for the Blades. Chris Guthrie had been brought in from Southend, supposedly to score goals, but could not cope at the higher level and a total of just nine league goals from him was just one of the disappointing aspects to this season. The opening day of the season saw us host the previous seasons champions Derby County and a 1-1 draw against this talented side gave no hint of what was to come. We lost our next seven games and our solitary point from that opening day game saw us planted firmly at the foot of the table. The optimism of the summer was now well and truly gone and I suppose I had been given my first lesson by the Blades, 'Never start to believe we are going to do well.' This is a lesson that I and my fellow Blades were to be given on a regular basis as the years went by.

A 2-1 win at home to Burnley gave us a glimmer of hope but that hope was short lived and two more defeats saw the board losing patience and sacking Ken Furphy. He had presided over just eleven games since ending the previous season so high in the table, but he was managing an aging squad and the board had decided to invest in the stadium rather than in quality additions to the team and Ken was now paying the price.

Rather than building a team around Tony Currie, as the chairman had apparently promised when persuading Currie to sign a new contract rather than be tempted by approaches from Manchester United, the board had relied on what was basically the team promoted in 1971 with seven of the 1970/71 promotion winning team still forming the backbone of the squad. Quite a few of those were by now getting well past their best and their potential successors were not a shadow of those players in their heyday. We now had a struggling team, a shiny new stand, that was to be half empty for years to come, and a debt that we were going to struggle to service. Excellent leadership!!!!

A 5-1 hammering at Wolves did nothing to steady the ship and when the board appointed Jimmy Sirrel, a funny looking little Scottish bloke who had taken Notts County from the fourth to the second division but had no experience at the top level, no one believed he would do anything other than take us to the second division as well. It was rumoured that he had taken a look at the books when he first arrived and had immediately wanted to resign; believing he had made a mistake in coming to the Blades. Just two points from his first ten games in charge did nothing to get the fans believing he was the answer to our prayers either. Sirrel was appointed in mid-October, but it was mid-February before he got his first win, 2-1 at home to Aston Villa.

Sirrel had signed a fellow Scotsman in the shape of 'Jinky' Jimmy Johnstone a former Scotland international who, in my opinion, was totally washed up by the time he signed for the Blades. I recall travelling to Leicester for a third round FA Cup tie where he performed awfully and I would swear to you that he was thoroughly pissed up as he stumbled about on the pitch that day as United lost 3-0.

It wasn't until April of 1976 when the Blades recorded four wins out of five games that United started to show any signs of the form that had brought them the relative success of the previous season and frankly by then it was far too late. During that run the Blades also gave us a reminder of that previous season when once again they came from behind to win 3-2 against West Ham. On this occasion I found myself ejected from the ground after running on the pitch, with my mate Paul Ayers, to celebrate the winning goal. I had also been involved in an altercation with a bunch of West Ham fans that had come on to our kop and were quickly shown the error of their ways. I don't know if it was the poor performances by the Blades or simply the fact that I was getting older but the next few seasons would see me attracted to the matches as much for the challenge of taking on the opposition supporters as for the prospect of seeing the team have any success.

The season ended with a 1-0 win over Newcastle and a 1-1 draw with Birmingham, both at home but it was all too little too late and we were relegated in bottom place. Our last six games had given us four wins, one draw and a solitary defeat away to Middlesbrough and we were again left to ponder what might have been if we could have found the form that provided that final flourish a little earlier in the season. Wondering what could have been was to become the staple diet of Blades fans for years to come

I suppose that my introduction to following the Blades had coincided with one of the high points in their history and I had been spoiled a little, but I was now well and truly a Blade and if that meant following them in the lower leagues then so be it.

The Long Fall from Grace
1976/77

The 1976/7 season was our first season back in the second tier and was truly unremarkable. Now without Tony Currie, who in an attempt to balance the books had been sold to Leeds United in the summer for what now seems a ridiculously cheap £250,000, we lacked any real class and Jimmy Sirrel could not manage to motivate the squad to produce any consistent results. Ian (Chico) Hamilton was brought in from Aston Villa and promising youngsters Keith Edwards, Tony Kenworthy, Steve Ludlam, Gary Hamson, John (Speedy) McGeady and Simon Stainrod were all given plenty of chances during this campaign, but only once during the season did we manage to string three consecutive wins together and we suffered hammerings by Forest, 5-1 away, Blackpool 5-1 at home and 4-0 at Chelsea along the way to a disappointing eleventh place finish.

The only real memories from this season for me personally were a 2-1 win away at Oldham over Christmas, where I was sick as a dog after eating a bit of manky pork pie on the coach on the way over the Pennines, and a 3-1 defeat to Bristol Rovers in the last match of the season where I got well pissed up drinking snakebites in a Bristol pub before the game and spent most of the match chatting up a girl working at a burger stall in the ground.

At Blackpool in November we were bombarded by house bricks, thrown over the fence that divided the kop, by unseen Blackpool fans and in March I received a gashed head at Burnley when again we were pelted with missiles. I don't know what is was about the Lancastrians but they just loved to throw stuff. Why could they not just come over and fight like everyone else?

It is a pretty poor season when your main memories of it are of feeling under the weather and getting hit by a brick!! I suppose the only real highlight was United finding a striker who actually knew where the back of the net was, with Keith Edwards managing to notch up 18 goals as we struggled to end up in eleventh place in a pretty dull season.

1977/78

The 1977/8 season started with Sirrel still in charge with his only real contribution to date being designing the badge that the Blades still wear to this day. That's how good a manager he was at the Lane, maybe he should have been a graphic designer instead; he seemed to be better at it than managing a football team, albeit one governed by a board of what appeared to be financial incompetents. Although even then I am not sure how original the badge design was as it seems remarkably similar to the Wimbledon tennis championship logo which came out around the same time.

We were not expecting much and poor old Jimmy seemed intent on living up to our expectations. With the underperforming Chris Guthrie having being offloaded to Swindon Town our hopes of getting the goals were put on new signing Bobby Campbell and the song made up in his honour pretty much summed up his contribution to the cause in his only season at the Lane '*Bobby Campbell hit the post, it should have been a goal,*' was the chant, sung to the theme tune to Bonanza off the TV.

With just one win and one draw from our first seven games and with the Blades languishing close to the foot of the table the board had to act and Jimmy Sirrel's reign at Bramall Lane was ended. Old Blades stalwart Cec Coldwell was put in temporary charge and six wins and three draws in his first nine games saw us elevated to eighth place and the fans were rallying for him to be made manager on a permanent basis. A series of decent results saw us going into the New Year in seventh spot but then three terrible results, firstly losing 5-0 to Arsenal in the FA Cup third round at Bramall Lane then league defeats 5-1 at home to Bolton and 5-1 away to Sunderland, had our city rivals fans taking the piss, joking that we were sponsored by the cigarette brand 555. I had to admire their sense of humour as the brand name was a perfect fit for the three results in question. The board however did not share the humour and swiftly appointed Harry Haslam as manager before the next game.

Haslam had led Luton Town to the First Division on a shoestring and I'm sure it was the shoestring part of that equation that held most appeal for the board. The ever smiling Haslam and assistant Danny Bergara built a rapport with the fans pretty quickly, contrasting with the unpopular, dour Sirrel, but with eight defeats five wins and two draws over the rest of the season the results were not as good as the song that the fans made up for the management team (*'Harry Haslam, Danny Bergara, Bibbely bobbely boo'* etc.) and a twelfth place finish, one place worse than Sirrel had managed the previous year, did not justify the smile that seemed to be permanently on Happy Harry's face.

On a personal note this was the season that I passed my driving test and bought my first car which opened up new possibilities for away travel and me and my mates made trips to places like Burnley, Blackburn and Notts County in my tricked out Mini 1275GT with the trips usually being more memorable than the performances. It was also the season where I managed to get myself arrested at Hull City on New Year's Eve and, even though I believe I had done nothing wrong at the time the police randomly pulled me from the crowd, a £75 fine had me being more cautious, but not necessarily any better behaved, at most games after that.

1978/79

For the 1978/79 season the board made the mistake of giving Haslam some money to spend. Players like John Mathews, from Arsenal and Steve Finnieston, from Chelsea, were brought into the team along with the mop headed Peter Anderson and the worst goalkeeper in Sheffield United's history (my opinion) Nicky Johns. To make way for this influx of new players John Flynn, Bobby Campbell and crowd favourite Keith Edwards were moved on. Also during the summer of 1978 the World Cup in Argentina had everyone focusing on South America and the Blades were no different. Scouts from the club went over to Argentina after being tipped off about a talented youngster that had become available. The scouts liked what they saw and, apparently, a deal was on the cards. Unfortunately the board baulked at the transfer fee being demanded, rumoured to be one million pounds, and told the scouts to look at other options. They eventually signed a player called Alex Sabella who was a gifted player but not in the same class as the original youngster they had been to see. For anyone who does not know, that youngster was rumoured to be one Diego Maradona. I wonder what became of him?

27

Sabella was paraded before the Blades fans prior to the 1978/9 season and expectations rose amongst the red and white hordes; will they never learn? Sabella's silky skills and dribbling ability were soon obvious to the fans, shortly followed by his ability to fall over whenever an opposing player glanced his way. He was probably just ahead of his time as his type of antics are now commonplace amongst professional footballers, particularly at the higher levels, but back then many fans were becoming concerned that he may have had vertigo!

With four wins, six defeats and three draws in the first thirteen games the Blades seemed to have started the season just as they had ended the last and fifteenth place in the league represented a worsening in form rather than the improvement that was expected after the spending in the summer.

Just two wins and six draws in the next fourteen games plummeted United to eighteenth position and the alarm bells were well and truly ringing. I can remember a few years earlier the blue and white team were in a similar predicament and the local newspaper, the Sheffield Star, ran a campaign to try and save them from relegation, but now there was nothing done to try and help the Blades in their plight. It's nice to know who your friends are!

Later in the season John McPhail was recruited to become Tony Kenworthy's partner in central defence, and was to show his prowess by smashing the ball clear over the new South Stand on more than one occasion (the only player I can remember managing that feat). One or two promising youngsters were featured during the season but in what was to become a blueprint for the future any youngsters that showed promise ended up being moved on for mostly modest fees, Simon Stainrod and Imre Varadi being two of those that appeared regularly under Haslam but were sold on without us getting the best out of them.

Les Tibbott was brought in from Ipswich and the experienced Bruce Rioch came on loan from Derby County and while home wins over West Ham 3-0 and Notts County 5-1 along with a 3-1 win away to Newcastle gave fans a bit of hope, just one win in the last seven games put the Blades in the bottom three and preparing for life in the Third Division the following season. At the last away game at Cambridge United a 1-0 defeat left United all but relegated and fans climbed the floodlights and ripped concrete up from the terracing at the end of the game. That may have helped the fans vent their frustration but did nothing at all to help prevent the drop! What had started out with optimism in the summer had turned out to be the worst season in the clubs recent history, but we consoled ourselves with the thought that playing in the Third Division should be much easier and things could not get any worse; could they?

1979/80

Despite getting us relegated to the Third Division in his first full season in charge Happy Harry somehow kept his job and led us into the previously uncharted territory of the lower leagues for the 1979/80 season. The wheeler dealer Haslam was busy in the transfer market again and Jeff Bourne was brought in as our main striker along with Len de Goey, Barry Butlin, Tony Moore and the exotic sounding Pedro Verde. Gary Hamson was sold to Leeds United (who else?) and Ian Benjamin went to West Brom in an attempt to balance the books. Sabella was also touted to Sunderland but the player turned down the move and stuck with us while he waited for an approach from a First Division side (Cocky little sod).

I had swapped my car for a little Bedford van and had started doing some of the away games as weekend trips, sleeping in the van overnight. While the level of football had dropped the quality, and fun involved in following the Blades away from home had taken a turn for the better and the next couple of seasons contained some of my fondest memories, despite some of the results and performances. I suppose a big part of following your team is the camaraderie and sense of belonging enjoyed with your fellow fans along the way, and it is probably just as well there was something there to keep me interested.

An average start to the season saw us set off with one win, one loss and one draw from the first three games, one of which was at Chester City where I went and can report that Chester's ground was one of the worst I have seen. Their kop (yes we went on their end) was made of wooden planks with piles of litter built up underneath which was clearly visible through the many gaps, it was a real fire trap. On the plus side there was a very good chip shop near the station. The game? Don't remember anything about that other than the 1-1 result.

Things then took a turn for the better with eight consecutive wins which put us at the top of the table. Although it was only the Third Division, being at the top was a good feeling after the tribulations of the last few years. A surprise home defeat 2-1 to Colchester brought us back down to earth but three more wins on the bounce gave us the confidence that the Colchester result was just a blip and we stood well clear of the rest at the top of our league. The last of those three results was a 2-1 victory away to Brentford and after the match it was bedlam. I had picked up a couple of punk rocker girls on the way home from the previous away game at Bury and I took them down to the match at Brentford where they proceeded to pick fights with anyone they could, real quality chicks they were! It goes without saying that I didn't take them again, they were a bloody liability. There had been a bit of fighting outside the ground when fans of some of the bigger London clubs had turned up to have a go at the Blades and afterwards a man was found dead. The police were stopping any vehicles with Blades fans in, with checkpoints spreading as far away as Toddington services on the M1. It took ages to get away from London, but the day after it was reported that the man had died of a heart attack and his death was nothing to do with the fighting, which was a relief to me if not to the family of the man in question.

The next game was against Millwall who were in third place and a 1-0 defeat at Bramall Lane followed by losses at Swindon 3-2, where we had a good weekend away from home despite the result, and at home to Brentford 2-0 saw things tighten up at the top. Losing to Brentford was particularly hard to take after we had beaten them at their ground only two weeks earlier. A 4-0 home win over Gillingham settled things down a bit and after a 1-0 defeat at Carlisle, we rallied with home wins over Plymouth and Southend sandwiching an away draw at Wimbledon. The Wimbledon trip was probably the best away trip of the season with hundreds of Blades roaming the West End in London after the game, and those results left us sat proudly in top spot as we prepared to face the old enemy at Hillsborough on Boxing Day.

We were odds on favourites to win the game and all the banter around town was not about if we would win, but more about how many we would win by. Everyone was up for it and we packed out the Leppings Lane end as well as having pockets of fans scattered around all parts of their territory. With our league position and the fact that we still had Alex Sabella in our team victory was assured; we thought.

The game turned out to be a complete disaster. They kicked lumps out of us, with our captain Mick Speight being carried off injured, and Sabella just about disappeared after the first couple of hard tackles. The rest of the team folded and almost every shot they had flew into the net. They won the game 4-0, a fact that we are constantly reminded of even close on forty years later despite having beaten them many times since. Even worse than the local humiliation, if things can be worse than that, the result was the catalyst for a total collapse in our season and in the twenty two games following the Boxing Day disaster the Blades only managed to win four more games. If the first half of our season had been the form of champions the second half was relegation form and it was only the good start that allowed us to finish the season in what was still an embarrassing twelfth place.

Regardless of this collapse we still took good numbers away from home and in the last match of the season at Grimsby the away end was packed to bursting. Despite Grimsby confirming their positions as champions with a 4-0 victory, and even despite Jack Charlton's blue and white rabble clinching a promotion that should have been ours, the Blades fans celebrated at the end of the game like it had been us that had gone up. The team came out onto the pitch and threw their shirts into the crowd and I managed to grab Dougie Brown's shirt and quickly sell it on for a tenner. If this was how a Third Division mid-table finish was greeted I wondered what would happen if and when we ever won something.

Maybe because of this unwarranted exhibition of celebration, despite our total fuck up of what had been such a promising season, and notwithstanding our natural pessimism we actually went into the summer with a belief that next year would be the one that we got it right. Will we never learn?

1980/81

The 1980/81 season began with a hope that we could repeat the start we had made the previous season and this time maintain it

31

right to the end. After all this was only the Third Division how hard could it be to get out?

Haslam shuffled the pack again with Stewart Houston coming in from Manchester United, Bob Hatton, an aging but clearly gifted striker, was brought in to lead the line and midfielder Mike Trusson was signed from Plymouth. The big shock though was the signing of World Cup hero Martin Peters with a view to him becoming coach then manager. Sabella got his wish when Leeds, yet again, took our most gifted player, but with the energetic local lad Trenton Wiggan being given an early season chance there were hopes for good service to Hatton and Peters. Three straight wins, 3-0 away at Carlisle and home wins against Chesterfield 2-0 and Oxford 1-0 were followed by a 2-1 defeat at near neighbours Barnsley before a 3-0 home win over Swindon saw us sat at the top of the league after five games. Six defeats in the next eight games however saw us plummeting down the table and starting to lose touch with the leaders even at this early stage in the season.

Four wins and two draws in the next six games helped steady the nerves as we climbed back up to eighth place, just four points behind leaders Charlton and we were once again given the faint belief that there was a way out of this division for us this time. Two defeats and two draws including an epic 4-4 result at Walsall set us back a little, but two home wins saw us going into the Boxing Day match at Fulham still only five points adrift of the last promotion place with half a season still to go.

It was exactly a year since our Boxing Day embarrassment at Hillsborough and although we only lost 2-1 at Craven Cottage the nerves were beginning to jangle a little as we prayed the defeat was not to start a slide similar to that of the previous season. Our prayers were answered in the fashion that we were now becoming accustomed to, a 0-0 home draw against Brentford and then four defeats in a row.

Haslam, whose health was failing, had had enough and handed over the reins to Martin Peters. How he had lasted this long I will never know. He took over from Jimmy Sirrel, who many consider to be United's worst ever manager, and consistently delivered worse results and league positions but managed to see out just ten days short of a three year term in charge. Sirrel by the way had subsequently returned to Notts County and led them to the First division in this very season.

Peters quickly proved, as others before and since have done, that winning a World Cup was no guarantee of being able to make the transition to a manager and his results, as well as his rather aloof attitude, did nothing to endear him to the Bramall Lane faithful. Seven defeats and five draws in fourteen games including a 5-2 thumping at Swindon on my wedding day in February left us going into the last two games perilously close to the drop zone. Don Givens had been brought in on a short term contract during that period and looked to be forming a good understanding with the ever willing Bob Hatton but we were still struggling to turn the draws into wins.

With the last two games being away to bottom club Hull City and at home to Walsall, who were also below us, not even the naturally pessimistic fans of the Blades thought that relegation to the Fourth Division could really happen and most were already starting to gather themselves up for another charge at Division Three the following year. Thousands of Blades went to Hull City's Boothferry Park stadium in anticipation of a victory that would assure our place in the Third Division the next season. The game ended in a 1-1 draw leaving us still in need of a point to survive.

After the game I, along with a couple of my mates, managed to sneak through the players entrance and we spoke to Tony Kenworthy, one of the few players who seemed to have both the skill and the heart required to play in the type of situation we had found ourselves. Kenworthy had not been selected for the game, with Peters saying he was injured and not fit to play. However Kenworthy himself told us he was fully fit and had wanted to play. We managed to confront the manager and asked him if this was true and he refused to answer, simply telling us to go away. He came across as a right pompous bastard and seemed to have very little passion or even concern for the club's predicament.

The result at Hull left us facing the prospect of a last day showdown with Walsall who were the current incumbents of the final relegation spot a point behind the Blades. This meant that just a draw would see us safe and ready for a fresh assault on Division Three the following season. There was a crowd of sixteen thousand at Bramall lane, including a large following from

Walsall. I went on the Bramall Lane end amongst the Walsall supporters with a few of my mates but we were spotted by the police and ejected from the ground. This was unusual in those days as many home supporters would go on the 'away' end and if there was any sign of trouble the home fans were usually escorted around to the kop, but not on this occasion. We therefore found ourselves outside the ground fifteen minutes into one of the biggest games in the clubs history. Short on money to pay to get back in we looked for anywhere that we might be able to climb back into the ground, but, finding nowhere suitable, we were left with no alternative but to run and hurdle the turnstiles, with the first one over wedging the turnstile operators door closed while the rest of us got in. In hindsight I wish I hadn't bothered.

With just five minutes to go, and with the match looking destined to end in a 0-0 draw that would save us and relegate Walsall, John McPhail fouled Alan Buckley to give away a penalty which was converted by the aptly named Don Penn. We were facing relegation to the bottom tier of English league football for the first time in our history, but just a couple of minutes later and with time running out we were awarded a penalty when a Bob Hatton cross was deemed to have been handled in the box. The crowd went wild and the prospects of getting the point we needed had taken a turn for the better. One decent kick of the ball from twelve yards was all that was required to save us from the drop.

Tony Kenworthy was our regular penalty taker but again had not been selected so everyone expected John Matthews, our nominated penalty taker for this game, to take the penalty. The crowd went deathly quiet and then mumbles started to echo around the place as Don Givens placed the ball on the spot. It transpired later that Matthews had bottled it and opted out of taking the kick and when Givens hit a soft shot straight at the goalkeeper our fate seemed to have been sealed. Moments later the final whistle went and the angry crowd spilled onto the pitch. Some Walsall players were caught up in the fracas and in an attempt to calm down the crowd the stadium announcer falsely relayed news that Swindon Town had lost, which would have meant the Blades had survived.

Moments later the crowd realised they had been duped and turned their attention to the South Stand where they tried to get at the announcer. It was a sad and shameful day in our history and poor Don Givens will always be remembered, and blamed, for the missed penalty that put us into the Fourth Division, but at least he had the courage to take it on and I have far less respect for John Matthews who cowardly refused to do the job he was being paid for that day.

The season had started with all the Blades fans praying for an escape from Division Three, but no one had expected us to be escaping it by the back door and that day will always be remembered as the low point in the memory of any Blades fan of my generation. Just five short years after being in the top flight we were now destined to play in the Fourth Division for the first time in our long history.

A New Beginning
1981/82

By the start of the 1981/82 season there had been big changes at Bramall Lane. We had a new chairman in Reg Brealey and a new manager in Ian Porterfield, the former Sunderland striker who had scored the winning goal in the famous 1973 FA Cup final victory over Don Revie's Leeds United. Porterfield had led Rotherham United to the Third Division title the previous season and was tempted to Bramall Lane by the offer of a long term contract. Goalkeeper Keith Waugh, defender John McAlle and midfielder Paul Richardson were signed and as the season got underway former striker Keith Edwards was re-signed from Hull City and things were looking good for an immediate promotion. As well as the changes at Bramall Lane there had also been a change in the rules of the league as well with the introduction of three points for a win, which ironically would have saved us from the drop if it had been in place the previous season.

Another change was to the kit and after two disastrous seasons wearing a shirt that featured a single red panel down the middle rather than our traditional red and white stripes we now had the stripes back. The rational side of me tells me that the kit the players are wearing cannot affect their performance, but when have football fans ever been rational? We all have our little superstitions and lucky charms and, for me, wearing the red and white stripes is one of the things that makes the Blades better (despite having being relegated on a number of occasions in the striped shirts). Now we were back in our traditional attire things had to get better. I for one was happy with the change although the away kit, yellow and brownish stripes, was hideous.

I was married now and, on the orders of the wife, I had stopped the weekend trips and instead, for most of this season, I hired a van and took several mates to the away games on a cost sharing basis. I costed up the trips based on ten passengers but for most of the season I was inundated with requests from many more to join the trips and so I made a tidy profit on most away trips. I was not the only one doing this and journeys to many away games this season were punctuated by sightings of similarly crewed vans transporting many of the thousands of fans we took to all of our away games in Division Four.

This was the start of a season in the bottom division of the Football League structure and the lowest point in the club's history and yet, even amongst this group of beleaguered, doubtful, naturally disbelieving ensemble of followers there was a level of optimism that I had not witnessed before. It was almost as though the fans were willing the team to succeed. Success was not immediate though and, after a 2-2 draw at home to Hereford United, two narrow 1 0 victories over Wigan away and Colchester at home were followed by successive away defeats 2-1 at Hull City and 1-0 at Stockport County which had us starting to worry again. The worries did not last for long though and nine wins and a draw in our next ten games saw us sitting two points clear at the top of the table. In three of those wins we had managed to score four goals including an epic 4-3 win at York City where I had managed to cram thirty five people into a VW Transporter van to get to the game. On the way to the next away game at Port Vale a similarly overloaded van had to be emptied of its occupants in order for the van to make the steep climb up Winnats Pass at Castleton as we headed to Burslem for the match; Oh happy days.

We managed a run of seventeen games without defeat in the first half of the season but in the middle of that run, after beating First Division Arsenal in a League Cup second round, first leg game, before going out in a second leg 2-0 defeat at Highbury, we suffered one of our most humiliating cup defeats when we lost 3-0 to non-league Altringham in an FA Cup second round replay after drawing 2-2 at Bramall Lane. Mike Trusson managed to get sent off in the game and while the football was immediately forgettable I remember the game because of an incident with a burger salesman. Altringham's ground was tidy but very tight and refreshments for the away end were provided by a bloke with a stall set up outside the ground who increased his sales by climbing up a pair of steps by the perimeter wall and selling his hamburgers and hotdogs to fans inside the ground. My mate paid a quite high price for a hamburger that tasted so vile that, after taking a bite, he pushed the burger into the sellers face knocking him clean off his steps.

Although we remained unbeaten in the seventeen games we could only manage to draw in five of the last seven of that run and in the next game we were thumped for the only time that season when we lost 5-2 at Colchester United and found ourselves in fourth place in the table, albeit with two games in hand over leaders Wigan. That game attracted the Match of the Day cameras in a rare foray into the Fourth Division and, as usual, the Blades managed to save their worst result for when most people were watching. Porterfield responded to this slight dip in form by signing Colin Morris from Blackpool for one hundred thousand pounds, in what proved to be a master stroke. Successive 4-0 wins over Stockport and York saw us reinstated at the top of the league, still with those two games in hand over Wigan who were now just behind us on goal difference. It was very tight at the top of the league with only two points separating the top four and we knew we would have to keep getting the results if we were to remain in the promotion positions.

Although we managed five wins in the next seven games the draws we got in the other two were enough to cause us to slip to third place. It was that tight at the top. The following game was at home to leaders Wigan who were on a remarkable run of seven consecutive wins and it was vital that we beat them to stay in touch. Wigan were led by player-manager Larry Lloyd, the former Liverpool, Coventry and Nottingham Forest centre half who had amongst his honours Two league championships, a UEFA Cup, three League Cup and two European Cup winners medals and although he was now in the twilight of his career he was still a formidable defender and was moulding Wigan into a very good team indeed.

There was a healthy crowd of over twenty two thousand at Bramall Lane on a Tuesday night in March and, as a result of Lloyd's frame being slightly heavier than when he was at his peak, pockets of the crowd were intermittently singing '*Fat bastard, Fat Bastard, Fat Bastard*' at the Wigan colossus, who in response was producing one of his best performances and had Keith Edwards well and truly in his pocket. The normally prolific striker was trying his best but could not get a sniff of the ball while Lloyd was around. Each time Lloyd intercepted a Blades attack small chants of '*Fat Bastard*,' would ring out but Lloyd was revelling in it and if anything was playing better than ever. Then with very little time left to go and with the Blades kicking towards the Shoreham end, Colin Morris picked up the ball and sped down the right wing. As his cross was delivered, the previously flawless Lloyd slipped in the penalty area allowing Edwards to receive the ball in a yard of space for the first time in the match. A yard was enough and, after Edwards had slotted the ball home for the only goal of the game, what seemed like the entire crowd erupted with chants of '*Fat Bastard, Fat Bastard, Fat Bastard*,' aimed at the Wigan man. I looked around the ground and there were even small children and little old ladies singing along with the rest at the top of their voices as poor old Larry knelt by the penalty spot with his head in his hands as the Blades climbed to within a point of his Wigan side, still with those two games in hand. Some moments stay with you forever!

The following Saturday we were away to Tranmere Rovers and disaster struck as we set off for the game. Rather than the hired van we were travelling in one of my mate's cars and before even getting out of Sheffield the car's cylinder head gasket blew and left us stranded close to where the Meadowhall shopping centre now stands. We had no alternative transport and were too late to get a coach or a train to the match so we had to miss the trip and instead made our way to the Limes Club on Barnsley Road where we listened to the commentary of the game on a transistor radio as we played snooker in the club. It was a testing game that ended 2-2 and only sticks in my memory as when we got our second goal me and my mate jumped up onto the green baize cloth and became probably the only football fans ever to be ejected for invading a snooker table!

The Blades remained unbeaten for the remainder of the season (part of a run of 19 games unbeaten in total) with highlights being a 5-1 away victory at Halifax, where the shale terracing that surrounded the pitch erupted in clouds of choking dust each time we scored, and a 4-0 away win at Peterborough, who were, at the start of the game, two points ahead of us in the table. After a couple of draws three consecutive wins against Crew, Rochdale and another 4-0 victory over Peterborough, this time at home, saw us going into the final game of the season at Darlington needing just a point to clinch the Division Four title. This game goes down as one of the greatest days out in the Blades history despite being at such a low level.

A van was never going to hold all the people that wanted to go to the game with our crew so we managed to hire a coach, which was a job in itself as virtually every coach company in Sheffield was booked up. We finally managed to find one available in Worksop. The A1 was bumper to bumper with Blades on the way up to Darlington and at a refreshment break taken in Catterick Village there were hundreds of Blades fans filling all the pubs and playing football on the village green. The attendance at the Feethams that day was reported varyingly as anything from 11130 to 12557 with over eleven thousand Blades said to be in the ground. Those figures are however nowhere near the actual attendance as thousands more Blades, me included, climbed over a wall and ran across a cricket pitch to enter the ground for free. There must have been fifteen thousand in the tiny ground and fans spilled from the terraces that were struggling to hold them and stood just a couple of feet from the touchlines throughout the game. Many fans were in fancy dress and conga lines sprang up around, and on, the pitch at regular intervals. The match was won 2-0 with Bob Hatton and Keith Edwards getting the goals. After the match there was a carnival atmosphere as we all celebrated the first step on the long climb back towards where we believed we belonged. United's team on that day was *Keith Waugh, Steve Charles, Paul Garner, John Matthews, John McPhail, Tony Kenworthy, Colin Morris, Mike Trusson, Keith Edwards, Bob Hatton and Jeff King.*

With an average home crowd of over 14800, almost treble the next best, and a massive away following everywhere we went we took the division by storm and most commentators at the time agreed that we belonged much higher up the Football League. If it were only that easy.

1982/83

The following season it was always going to be hard to compete with our Fourth Division title winning year and so it turned out. Chairman Brealey again backed Porterfield with cash for transfers and Kevin Arnott, Ray McHale, Mick Henderson, Terry Curran and Alan Young were all brought in. None proved particularly successful and during the season quite a few players were sold or loaned out in an attempt to reduce the wage bill. With Matthews already gone Hatton, Neville, King McPhail and Richardson followed and even new signings Arnott and McHale spent time on loan away from Bramall Lane.

We made a decent start in the higher division where three wins and a draw followed an opening day defeat at Portsmouth. For that first game at Portsmouth I drove down after finding the football special train fully booked up. My Mk 3 Ford Cortina got us there just in time to witness a 4-1 drubbing before having to make the long drive back. Our decent start found us in fifth position after five games and looking forward to another promotion challenge. The hopeful feelings didn't last long and three consecutive defeats without scoring a goal saw us drop to fourteenth place and the reality of being back in the dreaded Third Division started to take hold.

We could never really put a decent run together and, while two wins and three draws in five games settled the nerves, four defeats and a solitary point from a 0-0 draw away to Oxford in the five games that followed left us heading into a hectic Christmas period starting with a match against Doncaster Rovers at Bramall Lane in a disappointing seventeenth position. Two wins at home over Donny 3-1 and Orient 3-0 were separated by a 3-0 loss at Chesterfield in a fixture schedule that featured two games on consecutive days and three games in a five day period. At least we seemed to have settled the Christmas hoodoo and three wins and two draws in the five New Year fixtures left us in fifteenth position with games in hand over everyone around us.

After a couple of away defeats, to Reading 2-0 and Wrexham 4-1, We hit the best patch of our season with five straight wins lifting us up to tenth place, still with games in hand over most of our rivals. Although we were ten points off the promotion places, having games in hand and with three points for a win now being at stake, we were starting to pick up mumbles from the more optimistic fans that a late promotion charge was possibly on the cards. Could it really happen? Of course not; while our home form held up, with four wins and a solitary defeat from the last five games at Bramall Lane, we did not pick up a single point away from home and with our games in hand all been away matches zero points from eight away games saw us finish the season in eleventh position. During this period I became a dad for the first time and so while we were going nowhere in terms of our league position at least my new son Steve would be adding one to the fan base.

The fans were by now well over the euphoria of the previous season's achievement and our unenthusiastic performances saw attendances dwindling. In the run-in we recorded what was a club post war low league attendance of 7649 to watch a 2-1 win over Bristol Rovers. We were a little disappointed with our season but we had finished highest of the four promoted clubs and, despite the fall in crowd numbers, our average home attendance of 11764 was second only to champions Portsmouth. If only they gave out points for attendances.

1983/84

The 1983/4 season saw the signing of a player who was to become a bit of a legend over the next few years when Porterfield went back to his old club Rotherham United to sign centre half Paul Stancliffe. Tom Heffernan and Joe Bolton also came in to bolster the defence. Young and Curran were sold and in this season younger players Tony Philliskirk, Gary Brazil and Gary West saw more action. West being christened '*Son of McPhail*' by one of my mates due to his resemblance in both appearance and playing style to the older defender, although clearing the South Stand was to prove beyond his abilities. The return of Arnott and McHale from loan spells brought a new energy to midfield

A 4-0 thumping of Gillingham set the season off on the right foot and five wins and two draws in our first seven games saw us get off to our customary good start and head into October in fourth place, just three points behind early leaders Oxford United with a game in hand. Of course the Blades were never going to give us an easy ride and a 4-1 defeat at Hull slowed us down a little. A home win, 2-0 over Bournemouth was followed by defeat at Orient by the same score and a frustrating 0-0 home draw with the pesky Brentford who seemed to be making a habit of slowing our progress. Things got back on track when a 1-0 win at Plymouth followed by a 5-3 home win against Scunthorpe saw us consolidate our third position, just two points off the top now, still with a game in hand. Mixed results followed before a 5-0 romp over Southend United at the Lane. It was still tight at the top and with just three points separating the top five teams it was still all to play for as we headed into December.

A reasonable December, including a 3-0 Boxing Day win over Rotherham and a 5-0 New Year's Eve thrashing of Bolton Wanderers saw us enter 1984 still in the promotion places and hoping for a New Year's assault on top spot. Two away defeats followed by a tricky period that saw just one win in the next five games found us out of the promotion places and trailing nine points behind the leaders Walsall. Then in an amazing change of fortune the Blades then won the next three games, scoring eleven goals in the process including six in a 6-3 win over Orient, while Walsall lost three in a row and we were now back in the top three just three points behind the new leaders Oxford United.

Our hopes of taking the title suffered a deadly blow in the next game when the leaders Oxford beat us 2-1 at our ground and, as they also had two games in hand over us, our eyes were now firmly on the remaining promotion spots. With seven wins, two draws and just one defeat in the next ten games, a period in which Porterfield brought in Glen Cockerill to help link midfield and attack, we seemed to be comfortable in the third promotion place four points clear of our nearest rivals Hull City, although Hull did have a game in hand. During that run we beat Bristol Rovers 4-0 which was the seventh time we had scored four or more goals in a game that season and that was to prove crucial in the end.

With three games left, two of which were at home we needed two wins to be certain of promotion back to Division Two. That though would not bring the drama and anxiety that United liked to put their fans through and so the football gods decreed that we would lose our next two games while Hull won one and lost one of their next two fixtures. As we went into our last game of the season against Newport County it was too close for comfort and, even if we won, a victory for Hull, who were now just a point behind us and at home to Bristol Rovers, could see them going into their game in hand needing just a point to pip us for promotion. Before our last game against Newport we had an identical goal difference to Hull so it was vital that we not only won but won well. In the end it could have been worse as, while we only beat Newport 2-0, Hull had choked and could only manage a 0-0 draw against Bristol.

Our season was now over and we sat proudly in the third promotion spot, three points ahead of fourth placed Hull, but it was not finished yet. Hull still had their game in hand to play, away to Burnley, who were in mid-table and had absolutely nothing to play for. Our 2-0 win over Newport meant that Hull simply had to beat Burnley by three clear goals to overtake us at the very last minute.

There was nothing we as fans could do but sit and wait and bite our nails, or was there? The game was played on Tuesday fifteenth May 1984 and, rather than sit at home waiting for our fate to be decided over in the small Lancashire outpost of Burnley, thousands of Blades fans made the trip over the Pennines to Turf Moor. I have never seen any official figures but from my own observations of the three sets of fans that made up the eight thousand attendance there were definitely more Blades than Burnley fans in the ground and it was very close as to whether we had outnumbered the travelling Hull supporters who were there expecting to see their team promoted. All the talk in the newspapers was not of who would win but of how many Hull would win by and as the game started it appeared that even the Burnley players had been affected by the speculation as they sat back in their own half and waited for the onslaught.

It seemed like disaster was looming when Brian Marwood scored for Hull in the second minute and Hull totally dominated the first half with the Burnley players seemingly overwhelmed by the occasion. Hull threw everything at them, but credit to Burnley; by hook or by crook they hung on until halfway through the second half when Marwood got a second. It was twitchy bum time now as wave after wave of Hull attacks came in pursuit of the goal that would see them promoted, but try as they might the goal just would not come and, after the last couple of minutes seemed to drag on for hours, the final whistle eventually sounded. Brian Marwood was in tears on the pitch as the thousands of Blades fans shed tears of joy as our promotion was confirmed by the tightest of margins. With the goal difference of the two clubs being identical, it all came down to our greater number of goals scored, 86 to Hull's 71. Against all odds we were back in Division Two.

Stuck in Second
1984/85

We were now back in the second tier of English football, but the return had come at a cost. Reg Brealey had backed Ian Porterfield with the cash to bring in the players to get us back here, but, despite a small trading profit on the previous promotion season, large losses on the 81/82 and 82/83 seasons and large interest charges on loans meant that the club's belt had to be tightened and so we started life at the higher level without any significant signings.

Two wins and two draws in our first four games saw us in a comfortable ninth position, but having just scraped into the last promotion place the previous year it was clear that the squad was not strong enough to take the higher division by storm. Five defeats and no wins in our next seven games including three consecutive home losses and a 5-1 thumping at Oxford brought home the reality of what we were up against. A spirited 2-2 draw with top flight Everton in second round, first leg of the League Cup gave us a bright spot in the gloom, but in the return match at Goodison Park we were well beaten 4-0 as a good following of Blades fans could only stand and admire the Merseyside team's quality on the night.

One win and four draws in the next eight games saw us going into the Christmas fixtures in the relegation zone. In response to the poor results Porterfield had brought in veteran keeper John Burridge, for a fee, and Liverpool legend Phil Thompson on a free transfer to try and shore up the defences as well as adding another free signing, Mel Eves, to the attack. Denis Mortimer came on loan from Aston Villa and added a bit of quality to midfield and the results took a turn for the better. Two wins out of three over Christmas (we lost at Fulham on Boxing Day, which wasn't a good sign) settled the nerves and after losing 4-3 to Birmingham at the Lane on New Year's Day we put together a five match unbeaten run which saw us lifted up to thirteenth in the table.

Unfortunately luck was not on our side and Dennis Mortimer was injured playing against Barnsley bringing to an end his time at Bramall Lane and in the next game, a 5-0 hammering by

Wimbledon Phil Thompson suffered a punctured lung and his season was over too. To be fair Thompson never really looked like the player he had been at Liverpool. The remainder of the season saw some pretty shoddy performances and with Keith Edwards looking unsettled and suffering from injuries the goals dried up as we finished the season with just two wins and four draws coming from the last thirteen games. It was only the fact that there were four teams in the division that were even worse than us that we managed to finish in eighteenth place, seven points clear of the drop zone.

This was the season that I had first started to take my son Steve to Bramall Lane and it is probably fortunate for both me and him that at just over one year old he was oblivious to anything that was happening on the pitch. It had been a pretty poor season and, in a period where football attendances overall were pretty poor, with some of our home games seeing less than ten thousand supporters our average home attendance was only fractional over twelve thousand. This however still made us the fifth best supported club in the division which was pretty good going considering the performances and results we had to endure.

1985/86

When Ian Porterfield had been given the manager's job it was part of a five year plan to get us back into the top flight. The 1985/6 season was therefore the last of those five years and so, if the plan was to be achieved, we needed to be challenging for promotion. The previous season had shown us that the squad was not good enough and so Porterfield brought in Peter Withe from Aston Villa. The striker who had a Football League title and European Cup winner's medal to his name was seen as a massive coup for the Blades even though he was by then thirty four years old. Other new recruits were Ken McNaught from West Brom and Ray Lewington from Fulham. Porterfield was clearly looking at experience to bring the success we desired.

Prior to the start of this season I had taken the family, now boosted by my nine month old daughter Michelle to see the Blades play a friendly game at Skegness and after having his photo taken sat on the shoulders of Keith Edwards our Steve, now two and a bit years old managed to invade the pitch as United were lining up for a corner (took my eye off him for a matter of seconds).

Edwards scored in that friendly but was rewarded by being left out of the team for the start of the season with Porterfield opting to play Colin Morris alongside Withe upfront. The fans were not happy as despite starting off with wins 3-1 away to Stoke and 4-0 at home to Wimbledon the next nine results saw five draws and a solitary win 3-2 away at Fulham which left us sat in a mid-table eleventh position.

Edwards had been reinstated to the team and with Colin Morris now back in his accustomed right wing position and being pushed for his place by new arrival Steve Wigley the Blades form improved. With the side looking more balanced Edwards, Morris and Withe scored seventeen goals between them in a run of six wins and two draws that saw them move up to second position and it seemed the five year plan was back on track. This however was Sheffield United and so in response to the fans new found optimism they responded in their customary fashion and proceeded to lose the next four games in a row including a Boxing Day loss at Sunderland that dropped us to eighth place.

The wheels had come off again and although we managed to maintain some form at home we struggled on the road and performances were pretty poor. When we were beaten 5-2 at home to eventual champions Norwich City it was clear to the board that Porterfield was out of his depth at this level, having never managed in the Second Division prior to this spell with the Blades and his contract was terminated. We were however still in seventh spot and therefore had an outside chance of still making it into the promotion spots. What we needed was a dynamic, experienced manager to squeeze every last drop out of the players in the remaining nine games. What we got was Billy McEwan!!

McEwan had been youth team coach and was appointed manager until the end of the season. It was an uninspired appointment and resulted in an uninspired finish to the season with three wins, three draws and three defeats coming in those last nine games. What McEwan did do was to bring David Frain into the first team. I had worked with Dave before he left his job (and took a pay cut) as a plumber for Sheffield City Council to join the Blades in September 1985. Dave had been a very good amateur player and I had played alongside him in a few interdepartmental games at work. At the lower levels Dave looked like a man amongst boys and was outstanding in most games. Unfortunately as a new professional he sometimes looked like a fish out of water, possibly in awe of some of the players around him. He did however manage to score a goal against Leeds United in a 3-2 victory at Bramall Lane. We ended the season in seventh position and even though this was our highest league finish since we were relegated from Division One in 1976 I felt disappointed and went into the summer a little disillusioned.

1986/87

The 1986/87 season was one that we entered with our expectations low and not really fancying the Blades for any form of glory. McEwan had been confirmed as manager and that on its own seemed to confirm that Brearley's ambition to return to the top flight was diminishing. McEwan began to clear out some of the older players including Ray Lewington, Mel Eves, Joe Bolton, Tony Kenworthy and Phil Thompson and with Keith Edwards being sold to, you guessed it, Leeds United and Ken McNaught retiring due to injury the squad took on a younger look. The money from Edwards financed the signing of a few new players with Andy Barnsley, Mark Dempsy, Martin Pike, Peter Beagrie, Chris Wilder, and Tony Daws coming in. '*Who?*' Was the reaction to most of those signings.

The football was uninspiring and mixed results saw us sitting in mid-table for most of the season. Throwing away a 3-0 lead to draw at home to Reading was typical of United that season, although there were still one or two highlights. My mate Dave Frain came on as substitute to score a last minute winner at home to Sunderland when we had been ready to settle for a draw and in December a remarkable game at Bramhall saw four players sent off. With our ten players up against just eight from Portsmouth for the whole of the second half it looked like it should be easy for us, but we struggled to break down the Pompey blockade and it was only a late own goal, deflected in by Paul Mariner, that gave us a 1-0 victory.

Martin Kuhl was brought in towards the end of the season to bolster the midfield, but without Edwards it was a lack of goals that blighted this season with Peter Beagrie and Steve Foley sharing top scorer spot with just nine league goals each. I suppose it sums up the season if I tell you that the real highlight of this season for me was in October of 1986 when the Blades put on a testimonial match for Tony Currie. A Sheffield United eleven that featured many of our early seventies heroes played a Celebrity All Stars team put together by TV star Dennis Waterman and the Bramall Lane staff were caught off guard when, after expecting just a few thousand to turn up, they had to open extra areas of the ground to accommodate the seventeen thousand five hundred fans that showed up to honour the Blades legend. Currie himself turned out and, even with his crippled knees, managed to spray some of his trademark long passes around and Trevor Hockey, ignoring the 'friendly' status of the match, reminded one or two of the opposition what a proper tackle was. The game ended in a 7-5 win for Currie's Blades and was a very entertaining distraction in an otherwise lacklustre season.

This period was really hard for us fans and, while we were playing at a higher level than in the dark days of the Third and Fourth Divisions, the prospect of us being promoted was never even considered by most of our fans, who could clearly see the team's frailties and limitations. I suppose it is a feeling shared by the supporters of many other teams that it is generally a better experience to see your team winning at a lower level than struggling in a higher division and this season, where neither promotion nor relegation were ever really on the cards, just sapped the enthusiasm from many followers. I even tried giving the home games a miss but on the first attempt I felt weird not being there and rather like a drug addict going cold turkey I got the shakes and found myself heading for the ground and getting inside at twenty past three.

Billy McEwan will always be remembered as a dull manager at a time where United drew some of their lowest crowds, with the 86/87 season seeing an average attendance of only nine thousand nine hundred and eighty two, and the Blades played some of their least attractive football, but a ninth place finish, following the previous year's seventh spot, given the resources made available to him, still puts him, at this moment in time, ahead of Sirrel, Haslam and Porterfield in terms of finishing positions.

1987/88

1987/88 saw McEwan given a bit of money to spend and he spent it all on Richard Cadette, a striker from Southend United.

After the earlier failure of Chris Guthrie, signed from the same club, United should have known better, but if we had ever learned from our mistakes we would probably have not been looking for salvation from the lower leagues anyway.

McEwan also brought in goalkeeper Andy Leaning and midfielder Mark Todd, who came on a free from Manchester United. Having being the youth team coach it also came as no surprise that McEwan gave more first team experience to younger players like Duffield, Marsden, Mendonca, Philiskirk and Smith. McEwan was soon probably wishing he had saved the money spent on Cadette as young Tony Philiskirk outscored the expensive striker in the early stages of the season. Those goals were not enough to get the results though and with just one win from the first nine games the Blades found themselves second from bottom.

Four straight wins saw us climb back to a more comfortable eleventh position but then only two more wins in the next fourteen games, the last of which was a 5-0 home thrashing by Oldhan saw us in eighteenth place at the start of 1988 and McEwan resigned.

Danny Bergara was put in temporary charge and presided over an FA Cup win over non-league Maidstone United and a league victory away to Bournemouth. I went to the Bournemouth game, driving for five hours each way to watch ninety minutes of football and I did not even get to see the sea. In the stands at that game was a certain Mr David Bassett, who was subsequently appointed as our new manager and began his attempts to save the Blades with a 1-0 loss at Stoke City.

Bassett had taken Wimbledon from the Fourth Division to a sixth place finish in the First Division before a short and less successful spell at Watford where he was sacked before having chance to re-shape their aging squad into his own style of team. Bassett was, if nothing else, an honest, straight talking manager and right from the start he made it clear that the Blades might have to take a step back before they could begin to move forward and did not come bearing promises of an instant improvement.

With Fifteen games to go and no money available to spend Bassett began to re-shape the squad with lots of changes being made in a very short time. Bassett brought in his own man for the dressing room in the shape of Wally Downes who was a larger than life cockney character in the same mould as Bassett with the ability to make good dead ball deliveries, but was less capable in open play and his aggressive style led to two sendings off in quick time. Bassett's dealings also saw captain Martin Kuhl move to Watford with Tony Agana and Peter Hetherston coming the other way. The deals didn't end there and Cliff Powell, Simon Webster and Darren Carr were also brought in. Loan players Paul Williams and Graham Benstead were also added to the squad, but there were just too many changes in too short a space of time.

The season ended with the Blades in eighteenth spot, but there was still a lifeline. In the previous season the Football League had introduced the play-offs and, in those first two seasons, the team finishing one place above the relegation places competed with the three teams immediately below the lower division's promotion spots. This meant that United still had a chance to retain their Second Division status if they could win the play-off competition.

We were up against Bristol City in the two legged semi-final game and were faced with an away leg at Aston Gate just a week after the season had ended. I went down to the game with many other Blades hopeful of beating the west country side from the division below but in a tense game played in a very hostile atmosphere we narrowly lost one nil. The second leg was played three days later and a 2-0 victory was required. With the away goal rule still in play it was vital that we did not concede but the Blades, being the Blades, proceeded to do just that and went into half time 1-0 down meaning we would have to score at least three goals to get through to the final, as we had scored three goals only once under Bassett's leadership this was a big ask and although Colin Morris got an equaliser we could not add to the score and so our relegation back to Division Three was confirmed.

The play-offs had been introduced in order to keep the season alive for longer by giving more hope for mid-table clubs to have a chance at promotion. With a top six finish (after the initial two seasons) now being the target the seasons of many teams were kept alive for longer, often with up to ten clubs still being in with a chance of a play-off spot right up until the last game of the season. In theory this also meant that games remained competitive with fewer teams having nothing to play for in the closing stages. This has proved to be the case, but the system also has its downsides as it also meant that a club could finish in third spot possibly ten or more points clear of the nearest challenger and still not get promoted. It has also led to teams that could only manage a sixth place spot getting promoted which did not always make the division above stronger the following year. The biggest problem though was that getting into the play-offs was no guarantee of getting promoted and many fans have found themselves given that extra hope at the end of the season only to have those hopes dashed time and time again. Sorry if I sound a little bitter!

The Bassett Years
1988/89

As well as coming with the reputation of getting a pretty much unknown team into the upper reaches of the First Division, Bassett also came with the reputation of playing a no-frills long ball game and he had been given a lot of stick by the football purists despite his pretty amazing achievements. Having been brought up with the flowing football of the Currie/Woodward era I was a little torn. I craved for the kind of success Bassett had brought to little Wimbledon but was less than enthusiastic at the prospect of watching '*Kick and Rush*' football at Bramall Lane.

In the summer Bassett continued to bring in players to suit his style of play with the additions of Ian Bryson, Alan Roberts, Francis Joseph and a tall gangly striker from Doncaster Rovers called Brian Deane. Doncaster was a local club and the consensus among their fans at the time seemed to be that, with the fee reported to be around thirty five thousand pounds, they had done well out of the deal. Time would tell. Under the Bassett regime we had also moved on players such as Colin Morris, Peter Beagrie, Chris Marsden, Richard Cadette, Clive Mendonca and Mark Dempsey so the squad had a completely different look to it.

In pre-season Bassett played a blinder by adding a string of friendlies against some pretty poor Swedish clubs to our traditional pre-season trip to Skegness and in what was clearly designed to be a campaign to put some confidence back into the relegated squad we scored forty goals in just five games.

The 1988/89 season started with a 3-1 away win at Reading and a 4-1 home victory over Bristol Rovers and it seemed that the scoring problems of the previous season had been solved. A 2-1 defeat at Gillingam had us wondering if the good start was yet another flash in the pan before the next two home games had even the most sceptical of Blades fans starting to believe again.

The first of these games was at home to Chester City and I took our Steve along to see the new Dave Bassett team in action. I was still a little unsure about the prospects of watching United playing the long ball game that we were told we would have to endure under Bassett, but you had to give the man a chance. We stood on the kop behind the white wall where I had stood as a youngster so that five year old Steve could see the game and I am pretty sure that this game got him hooked in the same sort of way that the Cardiff game back in 1971 had got me. Bassett's style was to get the ball into the oppositions final third as soon as possible and then play the football from there. It worked a treat in this game and resulted in a 6-1 victory with Deane and Agana both scoring hat tricks. The following game at home to Northampton saw a 4-0 victory with Deane and Agana both getting on the scoresheet again and when Agana got another two in the 4-1 away victory at Brentford we had scored fourteen goals in three games and were top of the League. Give me this long ball game ahead of McEwan's 'purer' version of the game any day.

The next game was a League Cup second round, first leg tie against First Division Newcastle United and a 3-0 win was enough to see us through to the next round despite losing the away leg 2-0 two weeks later. The atmosphere and feeling around the ground, and indeed the city, was the best it had been since the Fourth Division title winning season and it felt good to be a Blade again after some pretty miserable seasons.

Back in the league a 2-0 defeat at Bolton interrupted progress before four wins and a draw saw us going into November still in top spot. A 4-2 defeat at Manchester City in the third round of the League Cup was followed by two away defeats at Huddersfield and Aldershot which were then followed by a scrappy part of the season interrupted by five cup games in the FA and Associate Members Cups. During one of those games Simon Webster, who had been having an excellent season, broke his leg leaving a big hole to be filled and Bassett, in what turned out to be another great piece of wheeler dealing, brought in Bob Booker from Brentford.

Everyone asked '*Bob who?*' and a little research revealed that Bob was struggling with injuries and had never really established himself at Brentford so Bassett's choice was met with some scepticism. Booker did not immediately look like our salvation but it soon became evident that what he lacked in skill he made up for in heart and endeavour, which always went down well with our fans and his attitude on the pitch was both excellent and infectious and lifted the players around him. Bob went on to become something of a cult hero at Bramall Lane and typified the spirit that Bassett looked to instil in his teams. The end of this tricky little period of the season saw us going into a Boxing Day game away to Notts County in third position and seven points adrift of leaders Wolves.

We beat County 4-1 and I thought that the Boxing Day omens that I had seemed to have got fixated on were pointing in the right direction. Unfortunately two defeats followed and, in another cup interrupted run of games in January, just one league win saw us starting February in sixth place, fifteen points behind top club Wolves (albeit with three games in hand). The cups were proving to be a distraction but after a fifth round tie away to Norwich, who were going well in the First Division, we got back to concentrating on the League. That game at Norwich was a great day out and thousands of Blades packed the away end with loads of inflatable toys (a craze at the time) being tossed around the crowd. It was a party atmosphere and even though we narrowly lost the game 3-2 we came out of it with a lot of credit and praise from many pundits at the time. Even my car breaking down on the way home did not spoil the day.

Now free of the distractions we set about putting together a decent run in the league winning five and drawing one of the next six games and climbing back into third place still with games in hand over our rivals. Good runs have to come to an end though and just one point out of our next three games saw us heading into April eleven points behind the leaders, now with just one game in hand. It was now clear that we were playing for second spot or risking the lottery of the play-offs for the second time.

Four wins out of five, three away from home, interrupted by a home loss to Cardiff saw us sitting in that vital second position with just seven games to go, four of which were at home. During this run Brian Smith had suffered what turned out to be a career ending break to his leg so Chris Wilder came back into the team at right back for the remainder of the season. With the fixture list looking favourable to us things were looking good. The Blades however were determined to make things difficult and with just one point from the first two of those home games we were left with tricky away games at play-off chasing Fulham, champions elect Wolves and Bristol City and just two home games against bottom club Aldershot and mid-table Swansea. It was going to be tight.

A 2-2 away draw at Fulham set us up for a nervous game against the bottom club with a narrow 1-0 win coming courtesy of a second half Brian Deane goal before a 5-1 thumping of Swansea saw us heading to Wolves five points clear of third placed Port Vale. Wolves needed just a point to be officially crowned champions but with a game in hand over us and a better goal difference they had, by all intents and purposes, already won it. With Port Vale playing at home to play-off contenders Bristol Rovers on the same night, draws at both games could conceivably see us promoted as Wolves took the title. All the clever money was on the 0-0 stalemate that could see both teams coming away happy.

The game turned out to be anything but the 0-0 bore that many were predicting and with a Paul Stancliffe goal giving us the lead at half time it was looking like promotion was on the cards for us and Wolves would have to wait a little longer for the title. An end to end second half, with thousands of Blades, including me and young Steve, packing the end behind the goal and willing the team on, saw a spirited Wolves team clinch the title with a 2-2 draw, but a Port Vale victory, 1-0 over Bristol Rovers, meant that we were still not actually mathematically sure of promotion. However a vastly superior goal difference over Port Vale meant that we drove home from the Black Country in a celebratory mood as we were sure that even the Blades were not going to lose a twelve goal advantage in the final game. The last match of the season was at Ashton Gate, where we had failed in the play offs the previous season, and although we lost the game 2-0 it was still a day of celebration as, even with Port Vale pulling off a 2-1 win away at play-off rivals Fulham we were promoted on goal difference with a nine goal advantage over Vale. With Brian Deane scoring twenty two of our ninety three league goals that season the thirty five thousand pounds reported to have been paid to Doncaster Rovers was looking like a real bargain now.

It had been tighter than we would have liked in the end, but that is how the Blades seem to like to play it. We had got out of the dreaded third tier at the first attempt and, with a team as prolific in front of goal as Bassett's men were who knows what the next season would hold in store.

1989/90

Bassett loved to deal and knowing that he had to pick '*horses for courses*' started to overhaul the squad ready for the upcoming campaign in Division Two. The 'Chirpy Cockney' had moved on defenders Andy Barnsley, and Steve Thompson and brought in David Barnes, Mark Morris and Colin Hill, improving the quality of our back line and with Simon Tracey having established himself in the number one spot at the back end of the previous season we were starting to look like a more solid side. John Gannon had also been brought into the team at the end of the previous season and he and Booker were to be the regular midfield throughout most of the season. Neither of these midfielders were ever going to show any silky skills but they were busy and combative and suited Bassett's style well. They were both aware of their limitations and so did not dwell on the ball, preferring to get it to the forwards as soon as possible. Gannon took time to win over the fans and his passing ability was not great but he buzzed around the middle of the park and won the ball more often than he gave it away.

The 1989/90 season started with a trip to West Brom and I took all the family over to watch the game which we won 3-0 with goals from Agana (2) and Deane, of course. A 2-0 home win over Ipswich followed and then I made the trip up to Middlesbrough's Ayresome Park to see a thrilling 3-3 draw. Agana missed this game but Brian Deane led the line brilliantly and though he didn't score himself he created havoc in the 'Boro defence and showed a level of skill and control that I had previously not noticed in the big fella. Other than Deano's performance the two things I remember from that day were the stadium announcer at Ayresome Park being very funny, doing what was almost a stand-up routine over the PA system, and our fans taking the piss out of the locals when, in reference to the Cleveland child abuse scandal of a couple of years earlier, they sang '*Get your kids out for the lads*' at the home fans.

The following game was a thrilling 5-4 win over Brighton at Bramall Lane, where after being 3-0 ahead we had conceded four times, but eventually won with a last minute goal from John Francis. We went on to record an unbeaten run of ten games to start the season and found ourselves three points clear at the top of the league in early October. A home defeat by West Ham, in a game we totally dominated but lost 2-0 was followed by another seven game unbeaten run and we still topped the league in mid-November. By now Bassett had added Carl Bradshaw and Wilf Rostron to the squad and a sustained promotion challenge looked on the cards. A 2-0 defeat at Newcastle United was a bit of a setback but two wins and a draw followed to set up a Boxing Day clash with Leeds United who had by now gone one point ahead of us at the top in what was starting to look like a two horse race.

A 2-2 draw with Leeds at Bramhall lane settled nothing and defeats by Blackburn at home and Oxford away rounded off a poor Christmas schedule. I nearly missed the Oxford trip as I called at a camera shop in Sheffield on the way to the game and got locked in a private car park by some knobhead with a padlock and chain. Fortunately, or maybe not for the padlock owner, I had a hammer in the car and managed to smash the lock off before heading to Oxford for the 3-0 defeat. Despite the poor Christmas period we still found ourselves five points clear of third placed Sunderland going into the New Year.

A six match unbeaten run in the league, punctuated by FA cup wins over Bournemouth, Watford, after a replay and Barnsley after two replays saw us still second in the table, now just a point behind Leeds and with a game in hand, and facing an FA cup quarter-final tie against Manchester United at Bramall Lane. The hectic schedule had seen Bassett add the rock hard Billy Whitehurst to the squad along with winger Paul Wood who eased local lad and Blades fan Carl Bradshaw out of the team towards the end of the season.

The cup game against Alex Ferguson's Manchester United was watched by over thirty four thousand fans and we did ourselves proud before finally losing 1-0 to the eventual cup winners with their goal coming from Brian McClair. I don't know if it was an anti-climax after the cup run, but we then had our worst spell of the season, losing four and drawing one of our next eight games. Despite those defeats, which included a 5-0 hammering at West Ham and a 3-1 home defeat to Sunderland, we still clung onto our second place spot. Wins over Watford and Oxford saw us going into an Easter Monday top of the table clash at Leeds United on equal points but behind on goal difference. It was being billed as a title decider and with just four games left after this one they may have been right. We had the chance to make a statement to the bigshots up the road and we did it in typical Blades style, losing 4-0 and probably writing off our title chances in that ninety minutes.

It was vital now that we did not let our season fall apart at the last minute and Bassett rallied his men to produce home wins over Port Vale and Bournemouth and a scoreless draw away to Blackburn which left us going into our final match at Leicester City level on points with leaders Leeds but just two points ahead of third placed Newcastle. There were several possible outcomes as we contemplated the possibility of winning the title with a Blades win and Leeds defeat at Bournemouth or the other option of missing out on automatic promotion if we lost and Newcastle won away at Middlesbrough. A win would guarantee us promotion, if not the title, but with Newcastle on a better goal difference a draw might not be enough. Anything could happen.

This was the season when United had the best away shirt ever, a fluorescent yellow affair that lit up grounds everywhere we went and sold thousands of replicas. On the 5th of May 1990 the shirts lit up Leicester as ten thousand Blades fans arrived in the midlands city. Many of those who did not wear the away shirts wore fancy dress and, in scenes reminiscent of Darlington eight years earlier, conga lines weaved their way around the ground. The normally pessimistic Blades were convinced we were going up this time and that confidence must have helped lift the team.

The starting eleven that day were *Tracey, Hill, Barnes, Booker, Wilder, Morris, Wood, Rostron, Agana, Deane, and Bryson.* Substitutes *Bradshaw and Whitehurst* replaced *Wood and Deane* before the final whistle.

After conceding an early goal United turned on the style, bombarding the Leicester goal and racing into a 4-1 lead with pitch invasions greeting the second, third and fourth goals and the police and stewards struggled to contain the joy of the Blades fans as promotion edged ever closer. Leicester pulled one back but a 4-2 half time lead was warmly greeted by the Blades fans who had all but taken over Leicester's ground. In the second half Agana added a fifth and the fans were on the pitch again but there was more excitement to come.

The final whistle heralded a 5-2 win which saw the Blades promoted and it took ages to clear the thousands of fans off the grass before the team could come out to celebrate with us. With the news coming in that Leeds had won 1-0 at Bournemouth we had missed the title on goal difference but finished five points ahead of third placed Newcastle who had lost 4-1 at 'Boro. The best news was yet to come though. As the stewards tried to clear the few remaining fans from the pitch the score line came through from Hillsborough where Nottingham Forest had won 3-2 sending our city rivals down to take our place in Division Two as we were promoted to replace them in the top flight. Could it get any better than that? The pitch was invaded yet again and the stewards gave up on their attempts to clear it.

After the players and Dave Bassett had come out and been stripped of their shirts etc. We all set off on the drive back up the M1 to Sheffield. With ten thousand Blades fans all heading in the same direction the motorway soon became clogged and the traffic ground to a halt. Rather than moan about it many fans got out of their cars and at one point I found myself involved in an impromptu game of football on the hard shoulder as the drivers who had remained in their vehicles honked Blades tunes on their horns. It was a surreal event and as the traffic slowly started to move again many yellow shirted fans leant out of car windows and sunroofs as we slowly headed back to Sheffield and the top division.

Bassett had gained back to back promotions and despite what his critics continued to say about his direct style of play he was hailed as a football genius in the red half of Sheffield.

1990/91
We were now back in the top division after a long, and at times painful, absence of fourteen seasons during which time I had started work, got married, had two children and moved house six times. There had been four World Cups since we were last in the top flight and football had taken a bit of a battering after tragedies at Bradford, Heysel and Hillsborough. A lot had happened over those fourteen years and a lot had changed in my life but the one constant over the years had been Sheffield United and now at last I was about to see the Blades step out as a top division club again.

There had been more changes to the squad over the summer with Bassett spending close on a million pounds adding Paul Beasley, John Pemberton, Jamie Hoyland, and Phil Kite to a squad that had lost Graham Benstead, John Francis, Jim Gannon, Darren Carr, Martin Pike, Simon Webster and Alan Roberts since the start of the previous season. None of the additions were what you would call household names but this was Sheffield United managed by Dave Bassett, not Liverpool, Tottenham or Arsenal and our cloth had to be cut accordingly.

We were hoping for a good start to the season and Bassett had once again taken the team on a pre-season tour aimed at boosting confidence and we had hit twenty two goals in four games against weak Scandinavian opposition. Poorer pre-season results in four games back on home soil brought the feet back to the ground and we were ready to go.

The first game of the season was a cracker, and definitely not the easy start that the team would have probably preferred to ease them back into the top tier. The fixture list had set us up with a home match to the previous seasons champions Liverpool. I had got season tickets for me and our Steve, who was now seven years old, on the back row of the South Stand and I have to admit that there was a tear in my eye as I watched the United players come out of the tunnel to face the illustrious opposition. After a first half stalemate the game went to form and we ended up losing 3-1, but to be fair no one was surprised and if I am honest I don't think anyone was expecting to pick points up from the top clubs, home or away, and our hopes for the season were more for decent results against the also-rans and, hopefully, a mid to top half finish.

The script for the first part of this season seemed to have been written at Hillsborough as game after game we plugged away but could not get that confidence boosting first win back in Division One. After gaining just two points from the first six games we were rooted to the bottom of the division with just three goals, all from Brian Deane, coming from the previously free scoring team. After giving long serving captain Paul Stancliffe some deserved games in Division One Bassett now let his head overrule his heart and released the old crowd favourite, bringing Morris in to take his place. Despite managing to beat Everton 2-1 in the League Cup third round we just could not pick up a league win and went into

November with ten games played and just three points in the bag. We were already four points from safety and most pundits had us as dead certs for relegation with not much more than a quarter of the season gone. Bassett had responded to the situation by spending nearly another million pounds, bringing in ex Wimbledon hard man Vinny Jones from Leeds and the talented but injury prone Brian Marwood from Arsenal. Neither had an immediate impact but at least we were shopping at the big supermarket now.

With just one more point from the next six games we were becoming a laughing stock and were sat at the bottom of the table ten points adrift of eighteenth placed Coventry. The next game was at home to Nottingham Forest and I think even the most ardent of our supporters had resigned themselves to an immediate relegation and possibly an embarrassing record low total of points. A 0-0 half time score line gave us hope that we might be able to pick up a fifth vital point, but then the game sprang to life and in our seventeenth game of the season we finally picked up our first win overcoming Forest 3-2 with two goals from Ian Bryson and the other from Brian Deane. Four days later we got our second win, away at Luton Town on Boxing Day with Deane scoring again, and after a not-unexpected 4-1 drubbing at Arsenal we won our third game out of four when we beat QPR 1-0 at the Lane on New Year's Day. Long standing Chairman Reg Brealey, who had been looking to sell his stake in the club, stepped down as chairman, being replaced by 'businessman' Paul Woolhouse. This was to start a period of instability in the boardroom, but more of that as time goes by.

Despite our little yuletide flurry, and despite the good omen (in my superstitious mind) of a Boxing Day victory, the reality was that we were heading into the second half of the season rock bottom and with just thirteen points to our name. The next two games saw defeats at home to Crystal Palace and away to Manchester City and the hope that had been raised around the Christmas period seemed to be forgotten. Bassett signed another one of his former Wimbledon players Glyn Hodges, initially on loan, from Crystal Palace and on his home debut he scored the only goal in a 1-0 win over Derby County. This was the catalyst for one of the greatest revivals ever seen in the top division and the

Blades went on an unbeaten run of eight wins and one draw that lifted them to twelfth place by the end of March.

Although the run was halted by consecutive defeats at Forest and at home to Arsenal the escape had been made and just one defeat in the last five games saw us end the season by beating Norwich 2-1 at home, in a game where the kop roof had been removed ready to make way for the new seated stand behind the goal, to end up in thirteenth place, twelve points clear of the relegation zone. The last Saturday away game that season had been at Coventry City and the Blades fans were in carnival mood again, after securing our top level status against all odds, and many were once again in fancy dress. At the end of an uneventful game many of our fans ran on the pitch to celebrate our escape with the players and a large number of Coventry fans ran on to confront them. I know it is frowned upon to condone any violence at football games, but I must admit that I watched on with some amusement as the Coventry fans were chased off the pitch by a Dolly Parton lookalike and a fan dressed as a gorilla.

As a fan watching the Blades that season I felt like my emotions had been through a mangle. The despair of those first sixteen games was crushing, but to then make the greatest escape I have ever seen and finish not just safe, but comfortably safe was just amazing and the best part was listening to the pundits, who had written us off even before September was out, changing their tune and singing our praises by the end of the season. The only down side was that while we were battling to turn our season around the blue and white team had somehow managed to win the League Cup and sneak into the promotion places of Division Two so we would be playing them the following year, but if you don't play them you can't beat them can you?

1991/92

After the spending of the previous season, and as a sign of things to come under Woolhouse's chairmanship, Bassett had little money to play with and had to wheel and deal once again. Morris, Jones, Todd and Wood moved on with Agana joining them before the year was out. Coming the other way was former player Clive Mendonca, Tom Cowan, Charlie Hartfield, who was to bring back a little of the psycho mentality lost by the sale of Jones, and Adrian 'offside' Littlejohn. We also saw the opening of the new kop stand and those fans with memories as long as mine were hoping the latest improvement to the ground would not bring the same fate that the previous one had.

The 1991/92 season started in a similar fashion to the previous season and, after a couple of draws, five straight defeats saw us, once again, at the foot of the table. The first win of the season came a little earlier this time with a 2-1 victory over Everton, but defeats at Notts County, Arsenal and Leeds were interrupted by just a single point from a 0-0 home draw with Wimbledon, so after twelve games we were bottom with just six points. During that little spell Bassett had seen defensive frailties and so persuaded the board to invest a club record seven hundred thousand pounds on Brian Gayle, another Wimbledon old boy. This deal started to raise doubts over chairman Paul Woolhouse's financial commitment to the club when the deal, in danger of collapsing, was only revived when Bassett himself made a personal loan to the club to help see the purchase through.

A 4-2 win over Forest at the Lane was a reminder to the team of the exploits of the previous season but defeats away to both Manchester clubs saw us going into a home Steel City Derby still bottom and low on confidence. The blue side of Sheffield, in stark contrast to our plight, were riding high in fourth place, but a derby is a derby and, as we had seen to our cost in 1979, form goes out of the window.

The game was played in front of a capacity crowd of almost thirty two thousand at Bramall Lane and was the first league meeting between the clubs for over ten years and the first in the top flight since 1968. The city was buzzing and with bragging rights been even more sought after than the three precious points at stake it was a game no one wanted to lose.

The Blades lined up in what I called their 'deck chair' shirts thin red, white and black stripes looking more like the covers of the seaside seats than football shirts, against our opponents in yellow shirts and blue shorts. The team sheets looked as contrasting as the positions in the league table with our collection of grafters, rejects and local grown talent lined up against their classy team scattered with internationals. The teams for that day were

Us: *Tracey, Pembertom, Cowan, Gannon, Gayle, Beesley, Bradshaw, Hoyland, Bryson, Deane and Whitehouse.*

Them: *Woods, Nilsson, King, Palmer, Warhurst, Anderson, Wilson, Hirst, Williams and Worthington.*

Brian Deane, who had been out of the side with injuries and glandular fever, returned to the team and was to cause plenty of problems for the opposition defence, but the man of the match for me this day was to be local youngster Dane Whitehouse who, after a stuttering start to his Blades career, was now starting to show what he was all about. A scrappy first half, where our determined defence and snappy midfield had frustrated our rival's attempts to play their flowing football, was coming to a close when Nigel Worthington floated in a free kick from near the corner flag. As the ball bounced in the penalty area John Gannon smashed a clearance into the air. As the ball dropped down from the sky John Sheridan and Paul Warhurst both ran towards the ball and collided in a comedy 'you've been framed' moment and Gannon, chasing his clearance played a ball over the top of their defence to Ian Bryson who took the ball to the edge of the box and smashed a shot towards goal. Chris Woods was up to his task and parried away the shot, but only as far as the feet of the incoming Dane Whitehouse who slotted the ball into the goal in front of the new Shoreham Street Kop. The first half ended just moments later and it was the red side of Sheffield that enjoyed their half time pies and Bovril the most.

The second half started with our neighbours pressing hard for an equaliser, but the Blades defence held firm and Simon Tracey remained untroubled. United looked to hit their opponents on the break and the better chances fell their way with Woods looking nervous each time the ball came into the box. A cross from Jamie Hoyland was headed towards goal by the energetic Whitehouse who was clearly up for this game and revelling in the atmosphere. The header was tipped over by keeper Woods and from the resulting corner Brian Gayle challenged for the ball which then dropped invitingly at Brian Deane's feet ten yard out. Deane turned and slotted the ball between wood's legs for the second goal of the game and the home fans went wild.

The Blades were getting more confident now and more chances followed with the best been a shot from Whitehouse that was handled on the line by Phil King but went unseen by the officials. Towards the end our yellow shirted rivals rallied a little and pressed us back but more solid defending kept the chances down and the biggest piece of action came when a frustrated David Hirst lunged two footed at Simon Tracey as the keeper gathered the ball. A mass brawl ensued with a dozen players in danger of damaging their handbags and it was probably the time taken to split up the players that took the referees mind of the tackle by Hirst and, having already being booked, he was a very luck player not to get sent off. Also lucky was Warhurst who in the closing minutes chopped down Ian Bryson as he ran clean through on goal. Warhurst got a yellow card, but in any game played nowadays he would have been sent off the field for his cynical challenge. The game ended shortly afterwards and not only did we have the bragging rights but the three points gained that day lifted us off the foot of the table.

Kevin Gage had been added to the squad and we followed up the derby win with another one away at Tottenham. I went down to this game by coach and it was good seeing all the Blades fans on Seven Sisters Road as we packed out a few pubs close to the ground. The game provided us with a welcome away win, the first of the season, but even so the game itself was unmemorable, I'd probably had too much to drink. The thing I remember most about this trip was the tricky walk back to the coach through some flats where Spurs fans were waiting to ambush us around every corner.

A tricky period followed where we only managed one win in seven games including an ominous Boxing Day defeat at home to Coventry and saw us still sat third from bottom after a 2-1 defeat at Liverpool on New Year's Day. In many seasons past we had been a team that started well and faded away, but now under Dave Bassett things had turned on their head and we were now starting badly and improving later and this season turned out to be following the same pattern.

A 4-0 cup win over Luton was followed by a league win at Southampton, where again I drove five hours each way to watch a match. This time I witnessed probably the best game midfielder Mike Lake played for the Blades, scoring twice in a 4-2 win at The Dell. A win over Norwich followed and then, after drawing at home to Charlton in the cup, I made the short trip to Forest where, in a game where Carl Bradshaw ran Stuart Pearce ragged, we won 5-2. The good form continued with a 3-1 cup replay victory over Charlton, played at West Ham's ground where our fans took the opportunity to pack out The Boleyn Tavern, something we would probably not have done if we were playing the Hammers. A 4-2 win at home to Man City ended a very productive streak which left us in fifteenth place which, although not by any means safe from danger, had us wondering what all the early season panic had been about.

The next game was an FA Cup fifth round match away to Chelsea and plenty of Blades made the trip down to Stamford Bridge. Vinny Jones was now playing for the Blues and we were wondering how he would play against his old team mates. We lost the game 1-0 but the lasting memory is of Vinny having a slight altercation in the six yard box as the players waited for a corner to come in and Carl Bradshaw pinning Vinny against the post, holding him by the throat. As Stuart Pearce had found out a few games earlier some players have a hard man reputation while others are just hard.

Back in the league a loss at Luton and a scoreless draw at home to QPR were the lead-up to the return derby match at Hillsborough. Bassett had once again dipped into the market bringing forward Bobby Davidson in on loan from Leeds and signing yet another of his old Wimbledon players in the shape of veteran striker Alan Cork. This was a night match on a 'Thursday eve' in March and again there had been a lot of hostile banter in the build-up. Their team were looking for revenge and their fans were looking for blood. I went for a drink before the game in a pub called The Crown near the dog track and even though the bouncer on the night was a workmate and knew I was a Blade he let me into the pub packed with their fans. It was clear pretty quickly that they were in a belligerent mood and I kept my head down in the pre-match session.

At the ground I found myself amongst the home fans on the kop as the away end had sold out quickly and the atmosphere was the most hostile I had ever known, and I've been in some very hostile atmospheres. There were Blades scattered all around the ground and fights broke out at regular intervals, spilling onto the pitch occasionally. After the Blades had walked out onto the pitch to be greeted by thousands of yellow balloons (away colours) the fighting was interrupted by the game breaking out and if the home fans were angry before the game they were not calmed down at all by the happenings on the pitch.

For reference, the teams that night were;

Them: *Woods, Nilsson, King, Palmer, Anderson, Shirtcliff, Wilson, Hyde, Hirst, Williams and Pearson.*

Us: *Tracey, Gage, Barnes, Gannon, Gayle, Beesley, Bradshaw, Rodgers, Davidson, Deane and Whitehouse.*

They were in third place and we had been struggling all season and a home win was predicted by virtually everyone. Except Bassett and his boys that is.

After just three minutes Deane broke into the box and cut back a ball for Whitehouse to tap home and give us an early lead. Things didn't get any better for them as they struggled to cope with United's breakaway tactics and when Bradshaw pumped a ball into the box, and Chris woods made what is technically known as a right bollocks of it, Bobby Davidson slipped the ball into the net to make it 2-0 at half time.

The second half started with the home team pressing for a goal and it eventually came from a free kick after Carlton Palmer had gone down very easily on the edge of the box. The kick was squared to Phil King and his shot was deflected into the net leaving Tracey stranded. The Blades started to get back into the game and there were a few naughty tackles with Palmer hacking at Brian Gayle, Shirtcliff and Anderson dropping Deane on several occasions and Hyde chopping down Bradshaw and getting the free kick himself to the disbelief of virtually everyone in the ground. Glyn Hodges came on for Whitehouse and then after Shirtcliff had given away a throw in, under no pressure, the ball came to Gannon who crossed into the box. Bobby Davison stooped in front of a static Viv Anderson and headed the ball, hovering just above the penalty spot, past Chris Woods to make the score 3-1. Davidson had not even completed his first game for the Blades and he was a legend already.

For the remaining twenty five minutes they attacked but could not break down a resolute defence and, after Alan Cork had replaced our new hero Davidson, Tracey made his only real save of the game as he blocked a good shot from substitute Jemson to deny them a last minute consolation goal. As the final whistle went and the Blades fans on a packed Leppings Lane end sang '*We beat the scum three – one*' in celebration of what was to become known as the 'Double Whammy' I strolled off their kop and headed home wondering why I seemed to be the only one on Herries Road smiling.

A 2-1 defeat at Manchester United in the following game could not dampen our spirits and we went on a nine match unbeaten run starting with a 2-1 win at Chelsea, in a game where Vinny Jones was sent off after just three seconds, and cumulating in a 3-1 win at Notts County. This left us with just two games to go and we had climbed to seventh place in the table. Our next match was against champions elect Leeds.

Leeds were at the top of the table and with challengers Manchester United away at Liverpool a win against us could see them crowned champions. We would love to deny them that glory but at the same time with the other Sheffield team in third place and still, technically, in with an outside chance of winning the league we did not want to assist in that unthinkable notion so from a fans point of view we were torn. The players however had no such doubts and went for the win. A good game saw the scores level 1-1 at half time and in the second half with the scores at 2-2 Brian Gayle, facing his own goal, managed to produce a delicate lob that left keeper Mel Rees, in for an injured Simon Tracey, stranded. The own goal confirmed Leeds as champions as Man United had lost at Liverpool. Maybe Gayle did have his eye on the Hillsborough clubs faint hopes after all!

The season ended with a 3-0 loss at Wimbledon leaving the Blades in a creditable ninth place, our best finishing spot since 1975 and a great result considering we'd had yet another bad start.

1992/93

The 1992/93 season saw some big changes. The First Division had separated from the Football League and had now been re-formed as The Premier League run by The Football Association. The remaining three divisions in the Football League had taken on the titles Division One, Division Two and Division Three with the old Fourth Division being no more. This was at first a little confusing as the second tier now had 'First' in its title etc. The Premier League was to get a much larger share of TV and sponsorship money and while the clubs in the top flight were happy with this there was some fear that clubs in the lower leagues may struggle. The Blades were in the top flight and remaining there was now even more of a priority given the financial incentives now on offer.

Another change for the new season was an update to the rules regarding back passes to the goalkeeper. To try and reduce time wasting by teams constantly passing the ball back to the keeper, particularly when leading in the later stages of games, it was now an offence for the keeper to pick up the ball if it had been played back to him by one of his own team. This was to lead to a bit of early season panic from some keepers and a few indirect free kicks in the penalty area with entire teams lined up on their own goal lines defending the set pieces, but it soon settled down and is now an intrinsic part of the game.

Prior to the start of the new season, with Woolhouse still at the helm, the purse strings remained tight with only goalkeeper Alan Kelly joining the club while Chris Wilder, Colin Hill and Clive Mendonca moved out.

The new Premier League kicked off on the 15th August, 1992 and we were at home to the previous seasons runners-up Manchester United. We won the game 2-1, which was a major surprise given our early season form of the previous two years, but the big statistic from this game was the opening goal scored by Brian Deane. This goal was the first ever goal in the Premier League and whatever happens in the future the names of Sheffield United and Brian Deane will be in the history books forever. Another lesser known statistic was that Deane's second goal was the first penalty that the Blades had been awarded in almost sixty league and cup games, which was remarkable considering the way we played under Bassett with the ball being hurled into the box at the earliest opportunity.

The first day victory gave us fans some hope that the poor starts were a thing of the past but United soon brought us back down to earth with just a single point from the next six games. Two wins and two draws steadied the ship but the team was dealt a blow in the next game when Dane Whitehouse broke his leg in a League cup win against Bristol City. Just two wins in the next eleven

72

games saw us entering the New Year still in the bottom three and in yet another relegation battle.

With it emerging that Chairman Paul Woolhouse had defaulted on his payments for Reg Brearley's controlling shares, Alan Laver was installed as temporary chairman on behalf of the Brealey family. Woolhouse was later declared bankrupt and, following fraud charges, disappeared and as far as I am aware is still on the run from the authorities. It was not a good time for the boardroom at Bramall Lane. We had been a bit of a laughing stock at board level a few years earlier when a bloke called Sam Hashimi attempted a takeover. The takeover fell through and Hashimi subsequently had sex change operations to become a woman and then back to being a man and the associated chatter clung to the Blades for years.

In the FA Cup a spirited revival after being two goals down at home to Second Division Burnley had earned us a third round replay at Turf Moor. A 4-2 win, with a hat trick from Deane, saw us set off on what was to be a memorable cup journey.

Another Deane hat trick saw off Ipswich in the League before a single Alan Cork goal knocked Hartlepool out of the cup in the fourth round and set up a fifth round tie at home to Manchester United. The cup was a distraction again as we lost three in a row before a 2-0 victory over Middlesbrough set us up for the next round of the cup against the Red Devils. A 2-1 victory with goals from Hoyland and Hodges put us into the quarter-finals for only the second time since 1968. Two wins and two losses in the Premier League including an out of the blue 6-0 hammering of Tottenham kept us out of the relegation zone, but we were still facing a battle to stay up as we went into the quarter-final game at Blackburn Rovers. A 0-0 draw saw us earn a replay at Bramall Lane which we warmed up for by losing 1-0 at home in the league to third placed Norwich.

The replay was edgy with Blackburn taking the lead twice and United's equalisers both coming from local lad Mitch Ward. It was still level at the end of extra time and the Blades won the penalty shoot-out 5-4 with John Pemberton smashing in the winner after Alan Kelly had saved from Wilcox. The semi-final draw was eagerly anticipated and we were drawn against the high flying team from Sheffield 6. The other semi was a North London derby with Arsenal set to face Spurs. The FA decided that, in order to accommodate the demand, the London clubs should play their semi-final at Wembley and, after strong lobbying from both sides of Sheffield, agreed that our tie could be played their too. This was a precedent that later became the norm for FA Cup semi-finals.

Our Premier League position was still precarious but a 3-1 win at Coventry saw us going into the cup game still just clear of the drop zone. I had been watching the Blades for around thirty years and at long last I had the chance to watch my team play at Wembley, the fact that it was against our greatest rivals made it even more special. Our rivals were again going well at the top end of the Premier League and with Chris Waddle and Mark Bright added to their already star studded ranks since the previous season they were odds on favourites to progress to the final. We in stark contrast were if anything slightly weaker than the previous year with, other than Alan Kelly, the tricky but inconsistent Franz Carr being the only significant addition to the team. We were going to have to defend well for ninety minutes and hope for a lucky break or two if we were to beat our neighbours.

Defend well was exactly what we did not do as the game got underway. A free kick was given away around thirty yards out and as I looked at the pitch from close to the half way line I was surprised to see that the Blades had not set up a wall to defend the kick. I was looking at our goal from directly behind the ball and it was no surprise when Chris Waddle took up the invitation to shoot and hit a curling shot into the top corner of the goal. One of their fans was sat in the row in front of me in the middle of the stunned Blades fans and the idiot not only jumped up in celebration but turned around and shook his arms in the air at the Blades fans. Unsurprisingly he ended up with a smack in the mouth and an escort out of the stand from an unsympathetic steward.

It was going to be an uphill battle from here and, after John Gannon had wasted a rare chance, with Waddle pulling the strings in midfield we defended wave after wave of attacks. Warhurst hit the woodwork twice and Waddle first shot wide and then had a shot saved by Kelly. United's only real effort coming from a Deane header which went wide of the post. Then as the first half was coming to a close Franz Carr won the ball and put Alan Cork clean through with their defenders caught off guard. Cork scuffed his shot from the edge of the box, but the ball rolled agonisingly slowly into the net with Waddle desperately chasing back to try and stop it crossing the line. Seconds later the half time whistle blew and we went in with the scores level.

In the second half our opponents kept on coming and we defended with everything we had. When the defences were broken we were rescued by Alan Kelly who saved well from substitute Hirst and again from Sheridan and Harkes and we hung on to a draw at full time. Our best hopes were now clearly resting on holding on for a penalty shoot-out. They pressed again and Kelly made an incredible save from Hirst before Waddle shot over the bar. After the first period of extra time we were still hanging on in there. In the final session of the game the constant pressure we were under resulted in a corner and some appalling set-piece defending allowed an unmarked Mark Bright to head in at an unguarded near post. That was enough and despite battling heroically against what even I have to admit was a much better team we were out of the FA cup.

I know we had lost to our greatest enemies and had been denied a first cup final appearance since 1936 but I did not feel particularly bad on the drive back up the M1. They were clearly the better team and there is no shame in getting narrowly beaten by a much better side and if I am totally honest I don't think we would have stood a chance against Arsenal in the final. Or is that just a cop out?

Our best cup run since 1961 was over and now we could concentrate on securing our Premier League status. A win, three draws and one defeat in our next five games saw us going into the last three games of the season just three points clear of the drop zone in nineteenth position so one last push was required and push we did. A 2-0 win at Forest, in what was Brian Clough's last game at the City Ground, saw the Nottingham team relegated and the Blades now looking for one more win to guarantee safety.

That win came in the very next game, away at Everton where another 2-0 win saw us climb to seventeenth position and with goal difference being well superior to third from bottom Oldham we were safe. With the pressure now off our final game was at home to Chelsea and a 4-2 victory saw us end the season in fourteenth place which did not really tell the story of a season that had seen us in or around the relegation zone all year.

1993/94

The uncertainty in the boardroom saw Reg Brearley re-taking his position of chairman and generating cash by selling Brian Deane to Leeds while Bassett was on his summer holidays. Bassett was not happy and predicted relegation, but was persuaded to stay in charge and brought in David Tuttle from Tottenham and a big blonde striker called Jostein Flo from Norway. Willy Falconer was bought from Middlesbrough but only lasted half a season before being sold on to recoup the cash. A couple of other bargain basement players came in, but didn't trouble the team sheet.

The 1993/4 season started with a 3-1 home win over Swindon Town, but we soon hit our usual early season form and could only manage one win in the next fifteen games. During this early season struggle another one of our better players, John Pemberton, was sold to, no surprises, Leeds United.

With Deane gone, Carl Bradshaw making the transition from winger to full back and Ian Bryson having returned to Kilmarnock pre-season an alarming, but unsurprising, lack of goals left us ending the year sat in twenty first place. The Norwegian Flo had been brought in to replace Deane as our main striker, but for most of the season he seemed to spend more time out wide, heading long crossfield balls back into an empty penalty area where he would probably have been better positioned himself.

Bassett had brought Roger Nilsen into the defence, but it was the lack of a cutting edge up front that was the real problem. Bassett eventually persuaded the board to spend money on a striker and added Nathan Blake to the forward line, but by the time Blake made his first start United had won only four out of thirty one Premier League games and were in the relegation zone five points off safety. Blake's arrival sparked a bit of a mini revival with four wins and five draws coming in the next ten games lifting us out of the relegation zone with just one game to go. That last game of the season was at Stamford Bridge against Chelsea who were in a lower mid-table position with nothing to play for. A win would guarantee safety and most pundits thought that a draw would probably be good enough.

In what remains one of the greatest bad luck stories in Sheffield United's history the Blades managed to turn triumph into disaster with just a minute of the season to go. With a 2-1 lead and just fifteen minutes remaining things were looking good and live league tables showed the Blades well clear of danger with five teams below them. Mark Stein then equalised for Chelsea, but with Everton being behind at home to Wimbledon no one was panicking. With just a minute of the game left the unthinkable happened when Stein got his second and Chelsea's third, goal and with no time to respond we lost 3-2. With Everton having turned around a two goal deficit to win 3-2 themselves, in a game that was later to face allegations of match fixing (and having seen footage of the goals it is my opinion that there may have been substance to the allegations), and Southampton getting a draw at West Ham we were down unless Blackburn, who were still playing, could get a goal against Ipswich and send the Tractor Boys down on goal difference instead. All Blades fans ears were on the radio and television commentaries as the Blackburn v Ipswich game came to a conclusion a few minutes behind the rest of the fixtures. History shows that Blackburn were unsuccessful and the 0-0 draw saved Ipswich at our expense and we said an agonising goodbye to the Premier League.

1994/95

The 1994/95 season was preceded by the demolition of the John Street stand, supposedly in order to make way for a new stand. With the Blades now back in the second tier building work had been put on hold and so we were once again playing in a three sided ground. The squad seemed to be in the process of being demolished too with Bradshaw, whose conversion to a right back had been one of the few successes of the previous season, being sold to Norwich. Cowan was also sold and with Franz Carr leaving in September without featuring in the first team the squad wasn't looking like one that would produce an immediate return to the Premier League and with Chairman Brearley openly looking to offload his shares, and a gaping hole in the side of the ground where a new stand was going to be required, the prospect of any meaningful investment was doubtful. Less meaningful investment had been made in the shape of two Australians, Carl Veart and Dougie Hodgson. With just one substitute appearance in the league

77

all season the rumours were that Hodgson had been bought simply as a companion for fellow countryman Veart rather than for his footballing prowess. Veart himself went on to score eleven goals in his first season but I doubt he will ever have a statue built in his honour at Bramall Lane.

A winning start to the season 3-0 at home to Watford was followed by what looked like becoming another of our trademark early season slumps when we lost two and drew one of the next three league games. A season where the league was our only priority was interrupted by our involvement in the Anglo-Italian Cup and games against Udinese, Piacenza, Ancona and Cesena added nothing but an unwanted distraction played out in front of tiny crowds. Fortunately the stutter at the start of the season did not last and our next seven games produced three wins one defeat and three draws to leave us in ninth place. After spending most of the last four seasons at the foot of the table (albeit in a higher division) it came as something of a relief to have an eye on climbing towards the play-off places rather than battling to get out of the relegation spots. However a fixture list that included trips to the likes of Tranmere, Port Vale, Grimsby and Southend reminded us that we were back amongst footballs also rans.

Three defeats quickly followed, just to remind us that our aspirations of making the play-offs were maybe a little premature before seven wins, four draws and just the one defeat in our next twelve games saw us going into 1995 in fifth place. An unlucky exit from the FA Cup to Manchester United left us able to concentrate on the league and our decent form continued with five wins, four draws and two defeats coming from the next eleven games and we were in fourth place with an outside chance of making the one automatic promotion spot with just nine games left.

This was a season where the process of reducing the Premier League to twenty clubs meant that only the champions would be automatically promoted and fifth place would be the last play-off spot. In the end the process proved to be irrelevant as unfortunately the loss of Mitch Ward, Brian Gayle and Charlie Hartfield in the run-in left the lack of depth and quality in our squad exposed and with five draws, three defeats and just one win, on the last day of the season, we finished in ninth place and eight points adrift of the play-offs.

1995/96

The 1995/6 season was to prove to be a season of turmoil on and off the pitch and the end of an era in the Blades history. With work on the building of the new John Street stand delayed yet again and with a proposed takeover by self-confessed Manchester City supporter Mike McDonald dragging on there was no money to strengthen the squad. Leeds United made another raid taking Paul Beesley to Elland Road and Adrian Littlejohn went to Plymouth. Some of the money raised by those sales went on Paul Holland and Mark Beard who came in, but had no discernible effect on the team or the results. A disastrous start saw the Blades losing their first five games and going into September rock bottom with no points.

Three wins and two draws in the next five games steadied the nerves and lifted us to eighteenth place, but four straight defeats saw us end October back at the foot of the table. A couple of wins in early November were followed by four defeats and a draw as Mike Macdonald finally completed his takeover. With United second bottom and the manager clearly disillusioned, lacking his trademark enthusiasm and seemingly unable to motivate his players any longer he resigned and the Bassett years were over.

McDonald wasted no time in bringing in Howard Kendall the next day, in a move which he had obviously had lined up prior to taking over, and making money available to transform the team, and with it our style of play. There were rumours that Kendall had a drinking problem but other than his red nose there were no outward signs of an issue during his time at the Lane, and to be fair I would defy anyone to manage the Blades without resorting to a drink or two.

Kendall backed by the new chairman was soon busy in the transfer market. Michael Vonk was brought in from Manchester City and Nathan Blake was sold to Bolton with Mark Patterson coming the other way. Hopes grew around Bramall Lane when Gordon Cowans was signed on a free from Wolves and, with a host of Bassett's squad being off-loaded, Chris Short came in from

Notts County and in the new year Don Hutchinson became the Blades record signing from West Ham.

Kendall was clearly building a quite different type of team to Bassett and while early results were disappointing a cup win over Arsenal lifted the spirits before Villa knocked us out in the fourth round allowing us to concentrate on climbing the league. McDonald's takeover was also the trigger to, at last, start the work on building the John Street stand. The changes continued with Flo's contract being cancelled and Hodges, Gage, Gannon, Tuttle and Veart all leaving and Andy Walker and Gareth Taylor coming in. Angell, Ablett and Muggleton also came in on loan.

The squad and style of play had been totally transformed but after a defeat at home to West Brom on the twentieth of February we were still in the relegation places with fourteen games to go. Kendall's new look team started to click and with nine wins and three draws out of those last fourteen games we ended the season in ninth place, just six points off the play-offs. Who knows what might have happened if only McDonalds take over had not been so drawn out?

A Managerial Merry Go Round

1996/97

After the good finish to the previous season and the improvements made to the squad by Kendall the 1996/97 season was one that all Blades fans were eagerly looking forward to. Gordon Cowans had quit the game at the end of the season which was a blow, but with the manager adding Nigel Spackman (player/coach), Lee Sandford and Petr Katchouro to the squad hopes of promotion, or at least a play-off spot were high.

The season started with mixed results in the League with three wins, a draw and two losses, but defeat in a two legged League Cup round two tie by Second Division Stockport County, conceding seven goals in the process, had Kendall looking to the transfer market again and bringing in David Holdsworth to strengthen the defence. After throwing away a 2-1 lead to lose 3-2 at Southend the Blades then went on a ten game unbeaten run to climb to third in the table. Two more wins in the next three games saw us in second place just two points behind leaders Bolton Wanderers, but bad injuries to Short and Vonk were a blow and results suffered with five defeats coming in the next ten games and we slipped to fourth place.

Jan-Aage Fjortoft was added to the team and Kendall also invested a million pounds signing John Ebbrell from Everton. With Nick Henry also coming in it was a signal of intent from the Blades. Unfortunately Ebbrell, who was signed despite there being some doubts over his fitness, was injured before half time in his first game and played no more part for the Blades. At one million pounds for less than one half of football that has to go down as the worst investment we ever made (I hope we were covered by insurance, but somehow I doubt it, this was Sheffield United after all).

With the Blades unable to get an away win in early 1997 it was the home form with seven wins coming in our last ten home games helping to maintain our position in the play-off spots. Vonk had been missed at the back and with no one managing to make the position their own Kendall added Carl Tiler to our defence for the run-in. Two wins and two draws in the last four games saw us end the season in fifth position and secure a place in the play-offs for the first time as a promotion seeking side.

The play-off semi-final was a two legged tie against Ipswich Town with the first leg being played at Bramall Lane. We led at half time after a goal from Fjortoft but Ipswich equalised in the second half meaning we would need to beat Ipswich at Portman Road or at least get a high scoring draw if we were to make the final on away goals, which were still used in those days. A mid-week return leg was strongly contested and when Katchouro put us ahead we could see Wembley beckoning. Kelly in goal got injured and could only hobble around as Kendall had gambled and had no substitute keeper on the bench. Ipswich took advantage and went into a 2-1 lead but Walker managed to scramble a goal to level the scores at 2-2. In extra time Nick Henry was sent off when he foolishly dropped his knee into an Ipswich player on the ground and we had to hang on desperately for the draw that saw us through on the away goals rule.

The final was at Wembley against Crystal Palace who we had beaten easily at Bramall Lane just a few weeks earlier and we were confident that we could do the same at Wembley despite having struggled away from Bramall Lane since a 2-1 win at Bradford on Boxing Day. Well over thirty thousand Blades made the trip to Wembley and it was the supporters in the red and white that seemed to be the most confident outside the ground before the game. Spackman was brought into the team to replace the suspended Henry and Tracey took over from the injured Kelly in goal with Nilsen in for Sandford being the only other change from the second leg tie at Ipswich.

Right from the start things did not look right with the game being played through a crowded midfield rather than attacking Palace down the flanks as we had done so successfully at Bramall Lane six weeks before. I personally thought that this was a tactical error and that Kendall seemed to be struggling to get the game plan right. This feeling was reinforced when he substituted Katchouro quite early in the first half. Our problems were then compounded when Don Hutchinson was injured and had to be withdrawn before half time. Without Hutchinson and Henry in midfield United struggled to get their game together and with Palace rarely threatening our defence the game looked to be drifting towards a 0-0 draw. Then with just a minute to go a hopeful ball into the United box was headed clear by Carl Tiler, but fell to a little ginger bastard called David Hopkin (I'm sure he was a nice bloke, but in recalling that very moment I must stand by my opinion at the time) who struck a superb curling shot into the top corner. With no time to respond we were destined for yet another season in the First Division losing our first play-off final in the cruellest of ways. Thirty thousand plus Blades made their way back home sick as the proverbial Skegness donkey as our first experience of a play-off final offered us hope, only for it to be snatched away in a moment that seemed even more cruel that the one that had relegated us at Chelsea three years earlier.

1997/98

By the time the 1997/98 season had started Howard Kendall had jumped ship and team affairs had been left in the hands of Nigel Spackman. Spackman had not managed before, but along with coach Willie Donachie was trusted to see through the signing of Greek defender Vas Borbokis, fellow Greek Traianos Dellas, Nicky Marker and veteran centre half Paul McGrath. Spackman also re-signed Brian Deane from Leeds and the previous season's play-off disappointment was replaced by new hope among the fans.

Unlike in many of the previous few seasons we set off like a house on fire and were unbeaten well into October where after a 5-1 crushing of Stockport County in our tenth league game of the season we stood second in the table four points behind Forest with two games in hand. After losing our first game 2-0 at West Brom We then went another eight games unbeaten, although four of those were draws and at the start of December we were in third place just three points off the leaders and still with a game in hand.

That first half of the season had been a revelation with the Blades playing some scintillating football with a wing back system that saw Borbokis and young Wayne Quinn raiding down the wings and supplying crosses for Deane and Fjortoft, who were backed up by Gareth Taylor to provide depth in the attacking options. McGrath had been excellent, marshalling a back three alongside Holdsworth and Tiler, despite his well-documented knee problems. Unfortunately those knees eventually gave way and McGrath had to retire from the game. Injuries then became a major problem with Whitehouse suffering a broken leg after a shocking tackle at Port Vale and with Vonk never regaining fitness and Quinn missing a chunk of the season we did well to maintain any sort of form.

There was a sign of things to come as, out of the blue, Mitch Ward and Carl Tiler were sold to Howard Kendall's Everton and although Graham Stuart came the other way Tiler was sorely missed particularly in the light of McGrath's enforced retirement. The fans were starting to mumble and rumours that Mike McDonald was looking to cash in were growing.

Although Spackman was allowed to bring in Bobby Ford and veteran striker Dean Saunders (who went on to score the cheekiest Blades goal ever when he took a throw in against Port Vale's retreating goalkeepers back and then slid the rebounding ball into an empty net) other players were sold with confirmation coming of moves for fringe players Mark Patterson to Bury and Andy Scott to Brentford. The biggest blow though came when in January both Deane and Fjortoft were sold on the same day with Spackman apparently having no say in matters. The fans were furious at this turn of events. With the Blades still in the play-off spots despite the injuries and missing defenders it seemed, to me anyway, that McDonald was doing everything in his power to undermine the manager and derail the promotion efforts.

When Don Hutchinson was also sold after the Blades had progressed to the quarter-final of the FA Cup it must have been the final straw for coach Willie Donachie who left for Manchester City not long after. Spackman was now left isolated, with his capable sidekick now gone and clearly no backing from his chairman he stuck with the task for a couple more weeks but resigned as manager on the second of March.

On the following evening United played Ipswich Town at Bramall lane and there were demonstrations on the car park outside the ground as fans called for McDonalds head. It seemed clear to the Blades faithful that he was operating in his own interests rather than that of the club and with the promising young partnership of Spackman and Donachie now gone, and with what appeared to be a fire sale of our best talent going on, our chances of promotion seemed to be diminishing by the day.

Two days later McDonald resigned the chairmanship although as major shareholder he remained as head of the plc. Kevin McCabe, a Blades fan, became chairman and Steve Thompson was promoted to acting manager. Although the match against Ipswich on the night of the protests was lost Thompson managed to rally the team and a draw in the cup quarter-final at Premier League Coventry earned a replay at Bramall Lane. Although we played well we were losing 1-0 with merely seconds to go and many of the crowd were leaving when David Holdsworth equalised. The game went to penalties and, thanks to a brilliant display from Alan Kelly who saved three Coventry spot kicks, we went through to the semi-final 3-1 on pens.

Thompson brought in Devlin, Hamilton and Chris Wilder and going into April we were still clinging on to a play-off spot and had games in hand over those around us thanks to the cup run. We had been drawn against Newcastle United in the semi which was played at Old Trafford and the Blades fans flocked over the Pennines to make up half of a fifty three thousand crowd that watched the game. Old Trafford is a famous old ground, but a word of warning, if you ever have the opportunity to go avoid getting seats on the first half a dozen rows. The pitch is raised well above the front rows of the stands and the view, with your head barely level with the pitch, is not great. There is no wonder the manager and substitutes sit in a raised area. The game itself was a little disappointing with the Geordies beating us 1-0 with Alan Shearer scoring with one of the very few chances in the game and, after another semi-final loss to tell the grandchildren about, we were left to concentrate on the league once more.

The turmoil off the pitch and the cup run had taken its toll and with an hectic schedule that included nine games in the month of April we somehow managed to stumble our way to a sixth place finish and made the play-offs on goal difference ahead of Birmingham. The play off semi-final was against third placed Sunderland, who had finished sixteen points ahead of us, and due to our lower placed finish the first leg was at home. Sunderland scored first, but goals from Marcelo and a cracking free kick by

Borbokis saw us heading to Sunderland's new Stadium of Light with a narrow lead. The Blades battled well but lost the game 2-0 to go crashing out of the play-offs 3-2 on aggregate. I could not get to the second leg game but watched it on TV with our Steve who was distraught at the end seeing the Blades condemned to another season in Division One on the same day he had been ditched by an early girlfriend. It had been a bizarre season that had started out so well and ended in yet more disappointment as injuries on the pitch and strange decisions off it led to forty one different players being used across all competitions. Once again we were left wondering what might have been if Spackman had been left with the players at his disposal to continue that excellent start.

1998/99

The 1998/99 season started with our fourth manager in just over a year coming in the shape of Steve Bruce who came along with the intention of continuing to play as well as managing the team. The squad was otherwise pretty much that which had finished the previous season. Bruce was soon to see that his introduction to management was not going to be an easy ride and with no money to spend, in spite of reportedly having been promised cash when joining the Blades, he had to bring in loan players to try and help the cause as the season progressed. Following mixed results under the new boss, supporters were reminded of the previous seasons shenanigans when Taylor was sold to Man City and Dean Saunders moved to Benfica well before Christmas.

Despite the lack of investment Saunders last game for the Blades saw us standing in fourth place after a 2-1 win at QPR. The following game, a 4-0 defeat at Sunderland also saw Steve Bruce make his last appearance for the Blades as a player. A now weakened United team struggled for results and just a solitary win against Huddersfield in the last game of the year saw us slip to twelfth place as 1999 began.

A couple of league wins followed FA cup victories over Notts County and Cardiff and the Blades found themselves drawn against Arsenal in the fifth round. This turned out to be a tie that I am pretty sure is unique in the history of the cup. The game was played at Highbury and the scores were level at 1-1 with around ten minutes left when, with Lee Morris down injured, Alan Kelly put the ball out of play so that the physio could come onto the field. When Ray Parlour then threw the ball back towards Kelly, intending to return possession to the Blades, Gunners debutant Nwankwo Kanu nipped in and crossed the ball to Overmars who put the ball into the net. The referee allowed the goal to stand and there was bedlam as the Blades players threatened to leave the field. The game was eventually restarted and ended 2-1 to Arsenal. Objections continued after the game and with embarrassed Arsenal players and officials not wanting to win the game in that manner, after discussions involving the FA, the result was eventually declared void with a replayed game ten days later ending in the same 2-1 score line in Arsenals favour.

Towards the end of the season Borbokis, Holdsworth and Stuart were all sold in an attempt to balance the books and the inevitable mixed results continued for the remainder of the season. Steve Bruce's first season in charge of a football team ended with the Blades in eighth position and the manager as disillusioned as the fans and to no one's surprise he resigned in the summer and went to Huddersfield Town.

1999/2000

The 1999/2000 season saw the Blades taking on a new look. Adrian Heath had been appointed manager and Dellas, Henry and Wilder were no longer on the books having been tagged on to the list of players who made the exodus under Bruce. Shaun Derry and Rob Kozluk had joined the Blades towards the end of Bruce's reign and the arrival of Shaun Murphy, Marcus Bent, and Martin Smith as the season progressed had the side looking fresher than the previous season. With Lee Morris and Curtis Woodhouse having broken into the team the previous year there was a more youthful look to the squad too. Unfortunately Morris had made an impression on others too and after playing just one league game he moved to Derby County.

The season did not start well with an opening day defeat at Portsmouth being followed by a home draw with Walsall before a newly promoted Manchester City side thrashed us 6-0 at Maine Road. After a 2-2 draw at home to Ipswich our season got started with two 3-1 wins, firstly away at Tranmere and then at home to Palace which left us in tenth place after six games. The form was all over the place and we could not put two more wins together.

Bruno Riberio was brought in from Leeds but had little impact, then after a run of six defeats in seven games that left the Blades in twenty first place the board realised that the novice manager was not working out and Heath's short reign was over. Russell Slade took charge for two away games at West Brom (2-2) and QPR (lost 3-1) before a new appointment was announced. Neil Warnock was to be our new manager.

Warnock was a self-confessed Sheffield United fan and after a nomadic playing career had had a similarly nomadic managerial career with promotions being gained at Scarborough, Notts County, Huddersfield, and Plymouth. He certainly seemed to know how to get a team up.

Michael Brown came into the team and in the first five games under Warnock's supervision four wins and a draw saw United climb five places in the table. Defeat at Walsall was followed by another five games unbeaten including a 6-0 win over West Brom at Bramall Lane which left us in a mid-table thirteenth place and more importantly thirteen points clear of the drop zone. Laurent d'Jaffo was added to Warnocks team, but, as I remember, his name was more exotic than his footballing skills.

Warnock had turned the Blades into a more rugged side and it was clear that no one was going to get an easy game, but it was clear that there was still work to do as United managed no wins and just four draws in the last nine games of the season to finish in a lowly 18th place.

No one was particularly sad to see the season come to an end. There had been few highlights as the board first went for a novice manager before realising their errors and turning to a man who had not only proved he knew how to get teams promoted but also had a deep affinity with the club and its supporters. We had seen three different people in charge of the Blades over the course of just one season and a total of seven managers (including acting bosses) since Howard Kendall had left in the summer of 1997. What we needed now was some stability.

The Warnock Way
2000/01

Warnock started to build his own style of team for the 2000/01 season and with the likes of Derry, Smith, Katchuro, Hunt and Marcelo gone the way was open for players including David Kelly, Georges Santos, Guus Uhlenbeek, Nick Montgomery, Keith Curle, Patrick Suffo, Peter Undlovu and Robert Ullathorne to make it into the first team over the course of the season. It was also a season that would see Phil Jagielka break into the team and there would also be a couple of cameo appearances for a young Michael Tonge.

Five wins and two draws in the first ten games saw us in eighth position and playing in front of crowds averaging thirteen thousand, exciting it was not. Getting knocked out of the League cup by our nearest neighbours did not help matters and indifferent form saw us going into the Christmas period in tenth place. At least it was a top half position and after last season's scare under Adrian Heath's management we were grateful to be three points off the play-offs rather than three points off relegation. Our spirits were raised by the fact that the blue and white side of the city had fallen from their glory days of the early nineties and were at this point in time sat in the last relegation place Two home wins over the Christmas period lifted us to eighth place now level on points with sixth place Watford and hopes were rising for a promotion push.

The New Year was not kind to us and four defeats in January, including an FA Cup exit at Southampton dashed the hopes we had had. We were still only four points off the last play-off spot but having played three more games than Birmingham our chances of catching up looked slim. A draw and then four straight wins followed and the first weekend in March saw us climb into sixth place and with twelve games to go it was all to play for.

Typical of the Blades, as soon as we had sniffed the scent of glory we choked and three straight defeats followed. A fourth defeat was something that we could not afford, not because of the league position, but because our next game was at Hillsborough and more than just points were at stake. The game was played on April fool's day which also just happened to be our Steve's eighteenth birthday so a present from the Blades was required.

United had signed Carl Asaba from Gillingham a couple of weeks earlier and also gave a debut to Darren Bullock who Warnock had signed on loan from Swindon. The Blades pressed from the start with Peter Ndlovu and Paul Devlin causing problems down the wings and forcing a series of corners before the home side started to get back into the game. Their team that day featured two players that would later go on to play for the Blades in Leigh Bromby and Alan Quinn, but Quinn was stretchered off with an injury before half time. It was a scrappy first half with the best of few chances coming from a Ndlovu header that went wide and a Murphy header being tipped over by the pie muncher in the home team's goal. Ullathorne was injured just before half time and was replaced by Guus Uhlenbeek for the second half.

The second half started with the home team applying pressure but then a long punt downfield from Tracey was chased by Asaba who shrugged Des Walker aside and laid the ball back for D'Jaffo to slot home the opener for the Blades. The game remained scrappy with free kick after free kick interrupting the flow, but, after soaking up a bit of pressure, Bobby Ford played a defence splitting ball out to Devlin on the right wing and his cross was glanced on by Asaba and crept past the fat goalie to put the Blades 2-0 up.

There were very few chances created as the opposition pressed to get back into the game until a bit of magic from Gerald Sibon who twisted away from three defenders and lashed home a left foot shot to make it 2-1. United brought on a young Nick Montgomery to stiffen up the midfield and, although they huffed and puffed, our neighbours could not trouble Tracey for the remainder of the game which ended with a Blades victory at Hillsborough yet again.

Asaba had given Des Walker trouble all through the game and with a goal and an assist to his name was man of the match in most people's eyes. Although Asaba went on to score five goals in his ten appearances this season and was instrumental in this victory over the old enemy he will probably not make it on to the list of the Blades greatest strikers, being remembered more for his regular off target efforts while at the Lane. An ironic chant that was heard quite regularly during his time with the Blades will probably be his legacy in many United fans minds *'When the ball hits the shop at the back of the kop, it's Asaba'* was sung to the tune of Dean Martin's "That's Amore".

The win at Hillsborough should have spurred us on for a grandstand finish to the season but it was not to be as we just could not get the run of wins we needed to push for the play-offs and with just nine points from a possible twenty four the season faded out to a tenth place finish. We were the top team in the city once more though, finishing fifteen points ahead of our rivals. Mind the gap as they say!

2001/02

Although funds were limited for the 2001/02 season Warnock continued to mould the squad into something more suited to his intended style of play. Kelly, Woodhouse, Quinn and Bent were now gone, with Robert Page being the main new arrival. After having had a loan spell the previous season, Paul Peschisolido came into the squad along with Shane Nicholson. While younger players Tonge, Montgomery and Jagielka became regulars as the season progressed.

Warnock instilled a battling style into the team and the disciplinary record of the Blades this season reflected that with seven red cards coming in that first full season under his leadership, with three of those coming in just one game. More about that later. Warnock was also gaining a reputation for his outspoken comments and his reported criticism of match officials did us no favours. I am a fan of Neil Warnock, but it is my opinion that his willingness to give his opinion, and the way he was portrayed in the media, must have left impressions on the minds of many referees who seemed to come to the Lane intent on giving decisions against us based on reputation rather than on what actually happened. This often led to Warnock making further outbursts and perpetuating the cycle. Watching his antics was always entertaining but probably cost us a few points each season.

This particular season started with five consecutive draws and a defeat which left us down in twentieth place after the first six games. Three wins and two draws in the next seven games saw us creep up to sixteenth, but it was not the start we had been hoping for. Just one win and one draw in the next six games saw us drop two more places and it was looking like Warnock was going to be no better than Adrian Heath had been. A draw at Wimbledon was followed by a 4-0 win at home to Birmingham and the Blades ended the year with a run of eight games unbeaten with a Boxing Day win at Bradford seeing us up in fourteenth place, eleven points clear of the relegation places.

Consistency was the missing ingredient and the New Year saw the Blades struggling to put a decent run together and hovering in mid table, with eleventh place being the highest position achieved all season. During that inconsistent spell we had a home game against West Brom who were in third place and looking like they had a good chance of promotion and this game turned out to be the one the Blades were remembered for in this pretty average season and for many seasons to come, though not for the right reasons.

West Brom were managed at the time by Gary Megson who had a history with our cross city rivals and was probably not on Neil Warnock's Christmas card list even before the events on the sixteenth of March 2002. The game did not get off to the best of starts with Simon Tracey getting sent off after just nine minutes when he handled the ball outside his area preventing the Baggies from scoring. With just ten men against a good Albion team we were up against it and West Brom took a deserved 1-0 lead into half time. With a man less than the opposition we were resigning ourselves to losing the game after Derek McInnes added a second goal just after the hour mark, but then it all went mental.

Warnock brought on Georges Santos, which was probably not the wisest move he had ever made. Santos had suffered a bad injury the previous season when Andy Johnson, then playing for Nottingham Forest, had elbowed him in the face fracturing his cheekbone. Johnson was now playing for West Brom and Santos took just a matter of seconds to gain revenge when he lunged two footed into Johnson, probably with the intention of breaking his leg, The referee had no option but to show Santos a red card and as a mini riot broke out amongst the two sets of players the red card was shown again when Patrick Suffo stuck the nut on McInnes.

We were now down to eight men and with Keith Curle throwing punches at McInnes soon afterwards we were lucky it was not seven. On the touchlines Warnock and Megson were also at it starting a feud that was to last for quite some time. The only surprise now was that it took the Baggies almost a quarter of an hour to add a third goal.

We had already used both of our allowed substitutes when, shortly after that goal, Michael Brown limped off with what was reported to be an injury and a few minutes later Rob Ullathorne also walked off with an injury which left the Blades with just six players on the pitch. The referee now had little option but to follow FA guidelines and abandon the game with eight minutes left.

It was suggested that Warnock had told Brown and Ullathorne to feign injury in order to get the game abandoned, but I am not sure why he would have done this as with the score at 3-0 and a replay being entirely at the discretion of the FA (and therefore being unlikely), and with the points dropped hardly being likely to affect our league status it would seem pretty pointless to do so. What it did do however was to give the press an excuse to have a field day and the game was reported with the headlines 'The Battle of Bramall Lane'. Other than the incident that blew up around Santos exacting revenge for personal reasons the game had not been a particularly dirty game, and hardly a battle, but the reporting attached a stigma to the Blades and to Warnock that was to last for years to come. Santos and Suffo never played for United again. Surprisingly United went on to win the next two games, but with three defeats in the final four games we ended the season in an unremarkable thirteenth place.

2002/03

The 2002/03 season was one that no Blades fan was looking forward to with any expectation of success, but, just as the Blades are capable of disappointing and frustrating us, they are also capable of surprising and delighting us. That's what makes being a Blade so interesting. With naughty boys Santos and Suffo having been shown the door Warnock had also said goodbye to several other players since the start of the previous season with the likes of Ford, Curle, D'Jaffo, Uhlenbeek, Devlin and Sandford having gone, leaving room for additions to the squad in the way of new

93

keeper Paddy Kenny, midfield veteran Stuart McCall and gangling striker Wayne Allison. Allison's signing was greeted by a comment in the local media '*If Wayne Allison is the answer then what the hell is the question?*' but he was to go on to prove his doubters wrong.

During a season that was to see thirty four different players used in the league campaign the Blades also saw new signings or loanees in the shape of Steve Kabba, Dean Windass, John-Paul McGovern, John Curtis, Steven Yates, Jon Harley, Owen Morrison, and at least nine others on the payroll at some point in the season. Warnock certainly liked to freshen up his squad.

The season started off steadily and after ten games we had won five, drawn three and lost just two and we were in an unaccustomed fifth position. Unfortunately one of the games we lost was to our city rivals in a game where we absolutely battered them, but contrived to lose 2-0. As the season unfolded it turned out to be of little consequence to us and of little help to them so I am not going to lose any sleep over it. We had also progressed in the League Cup overcoming York City.

After losing to Watford in the league we made further progress in the cup beating Wycome Wanderers 4-1 and then three wins and a draw saw us sat in fourth place. Two away defeats at Derby and Forest slowed us down a bit but in the next round of the League Cup we played Premier League Leeds United in a game at Bramall Lane and suddenly talk of a cup run was in the air.

Leeds put us under early pressure and forced an own goal from Blades defender Steve Yates and it was looking ominous, United's only real effort of the first half was a shot from McCall from about forty yards that was comfortably saved. Leeds attacked us again, but only a shot from Viduka that was saved by Kenny really troubled us in the remainder of the first half.

In the second half The Blades attacked with a little more urgency but a free kick curled just wide by Tonge was the only early effort. Allison was then put through on goal by Tonge who was starting to trouble the Leeds defence but the big strikers shot was blocked by Robinson in the Leeds goal. Peschisolido was introduced and immediately started to cause problems for Leeds with a cutback to Brown forcing another save from the Leeds keeper. In a rare attack Viduka forced a save from Kenny when it looked like he might wrap the game up for Leeds.

Ndlovu was brought on as the Blades pushed for a late equaliser and as the game went into stoppage time Tonge again sped past the Leeds defenders to put a cross into the box. The cross was headed away, but only as far as Jagielka who took the dropping ball on his chest and then rifled a shot into the far corner of the net from thirty five yards out. Then before the crowd had time to settle down and think about a replay the two substitutes Ndlovu and Pechicsolido combined and when Ndlovu's initial shot hit Allison on the back a Leeds defender could only manage to knock the ball back into Ndlovu's path and he slotted the ball home for the most dramatic of winners.

That win over Premier League opposition seemed to fill the Blades with confidence and a draw and two wins including a 5-0 away victory at Bradford City set us up for the next round of the League Cup, at home again, this time to Premier League bottom club Sunderland. The Wearsiders brought their poor league form to the Lane and the Blades dominated a first half which saw efforts from Murphy, Asaba and Tonge go close and the Sunderland keeper had to make a save when a Ndlovu cross was almost deflected into his own goal by a Sunderland defender.

In the second half the Blades continued to press and took the lead when a cross from Jagielka took a slight deflection and looked to be going into the net. A Sunderland defender hacked the ball off the line onto the crossbar but the ball bounced down to the feet of Murphy who could not miss from less than a yard out. Two minutes later a free kick from Brown was delivered short to Ndlovu and his cross was met on the far post by Allison who headed the second and sent the Blades through to the next round.

Back in the League the Blades extended their unbeaten run as a draw at Leicester was followed by a 2-0 win at Reading. This set us up for the next round of the League Cup where the draw had pitted us against Crystal palace at Bramall Lane.

The Blades were in a confident mood at home to fellow Division One side Palace and pressed from the start with Wayne (The Chief) Allison going close with an early effort. A corner from Tonge saw a Shaun Murphy header tipped over the bar and another corner was then headed back across the box for Asaba to put the Blades in front, prodding home from three yards out. At the start of the second half it was end to end stuff as Palace pressed for an equaliser. Then after a great dribble in the box a cross from Tonge was blocked by a defender as The Chief waited by the far post for a tap in. As Palace pushed for a leveller Kenny made a good save from Julian Gray before we succumbed to the pressure and a cross from the left side was turned into his own net by Shaun Murphy to make it 1-1.

The Blades responded immediately and after another dribble into the box Tonge found Ndlovu who crossed for Peschisolido, on in place of Asaba, to flick his header into the net and restore the lead. Pesky looked so far offside it was untrue, but the flag stayed down and the Blades took the slice of luck and a 2-1 lead. There was no luck involved as Pesky got his second and United's third when a long ball forwards was knocked down by Allison and the little Canadian slipped between two palace defenders to score from six yards and put the Blades into the League Cup Semi-final for the first time.

It was all eyes back on the league again as we went into a busy Christmas schedule with two wins and a draw extending our unbeaten run to eight games and saw us go into the New Year in third position. Portsmouth and Leicester looked to be running away with the automatic promotion positions, so a play-off spot was probably our most realistic hope for success. There was no let-up in our schedule as we now faced an FA Cup third round tie against Cheltenham Town, which we won 4-0, before our League Cup semi-final first leg game against Liverpool at Bramall Lane.

Thirty thousand packed into Bramall Lane for the game, but I was not among them as I was on holiday in the Maldives. Although I could not see the game my mind was on anything but the sun, sea and snorkelling as I kept logging onto the internet for updates. I must have had my fellow holiday makers wondering what was going on when at the final whistle I went berserk as the news came through that the Blades had beaten the Merseyside giants 2-1 with two goals from Michael Tonge cancelling out Mellor's goal for Liverpool. My holiday also saw me miss league wins 2-1 over Portsmouth away and 3-1 over our old enemy at home. Why had I decided to go away in the middle of the best season we had had for years?

I returned home in time for the second leg of our League Cup semi-final against Liverpool. I had been unable to acquire tickets and so missed going to Anfield for the closely contested game in which the Blades took Liverpool into extra time before a Michael Owen goal secured a 2-0 win which took Liverpool through 3-2 on aggregate. I was a little disappointed that we had missed out on a cup final against Manchester United, but I was not sure if losing in a final would have been better or worse than losing the semi. The chance to find out might have been good though.

The disappointment didn't last too long though as a 4-3 victory against Ipswich in the fourth round of the FA cup had us wondering if a cup final spot might be attainable through another route and when the draw for the fifth round put us at home for the eighth time that season against Walsall anything seemed possible.

We had extended our unbeaten run in the League to ten games but the cup exploits seemed to be taking their toll and we were beaten in the next four Division One games which saw us drop down to fifth place in the table. We had however, in the middle of this run, beaten Walsall 2-0 in the cup to set up a quarter-final tie, at home to Leeds United.

Having beaten Leeds already in the League Cup run we were confident of doing it again and in a tight game we had the better of the chances, but it was still 0-0 with just a quarter of an hour to go. Then a weak effort from Tonge was blocked by Danny Mills when he could have let it run through to the keeper and January signing Steve Kabba pounced to score in front of a packed kop. Brown nearly increased the lead with a carefully rehearsed free kick which Robinson managed to tip over the bar before the game ended in confusion. Kabba had burst down the wing and was chopped down by a Leeds defender and when the referee blew the whistle everyone was expecting a free kick to be taken, but the referee calmly picked up the ball and walked towards the tunnel indicating that the game was over and the Blades were through to their second semi-final in the same season.

It was now time to concentrate on the league and three wins and three draws in the next six games saw us climb back up to third place. The next game was a defeat at Wimbledon in a game where the players may have had one eye on the FA Cup semi-final against Arsenal which was next up.

The semi was played at Old Trafford and once again the masses of Blades fans made the short journey over the Pennines, this time to see their team take on the Gooners. No one had given us a chance against Arsenal but a spirited performance saw us doing well with The Chief giving their defence all sorts of problems. The game was won by Arsenal under somewhat controversial circumstances when the referee failed to give a free kick for what was later shown to be a clear foul on Wayne Allison and then, as Arsenal broke away, the ref clattered into Michael Tonge preventing the Blades man from getting to the ball. Arsenal continued up field and after a scramble in the area Freddie Ljundberg scored what turned out to be the only goal of the game.

Even then the Blades can consider themselves unlucky not to have got back on level terms when David Seaman made probably the best save I have ever seen (and I saw Gordon Banks' save from Pele in 1970) when he somehow managed to claw away a Peschisolido header from right off the line. I have watched replays of that save many times, including having a look again as I am writing this, and I still can't believe he managed to save it. So, with only the league left now, we headed into the back end of the season with second placed Leicester City thirteen points clear of us with just six games to go and our only aim now was to try and gain promotion through the play-offs.

Our next game was a 1-0 win over fellow play-off contenders Nottingham Forest and although we lost the following game 2-0 at Preston, a 2-1 Easter Monday victory over already promoted Leicester City combined with Rotherham beating Ipswich Town meant that our play-off spot was assured with three games to go.

I would presume it is always a dilemma for any team in that position whether to go all out in the final three games, maintaining form, but possibly risking injuries or suspensions, or to rest players, hold back and prepare to start again in the play-offs themselves. If we had strung a run of wins together and just crept into sixth spot the team would probably have picked itself and the play-offs would have formed part of an uninterrupted sequence of games. As it was we were going into the last three games just biding our time and the only thing to play for was possible making sure we finished third or fourth, thereby ensuring a home second leg in the play-off semi-finals. Those next three games ended in a draw, a win and a defeat leaving us facing sixth place Nottingham Forest in the semi with the first leg at the City Ground.

So we were in the play-offs, but as we had found out twice before that is only half the job done and promotion was by no means assured, but if it was all to come undone at least we had the satisfaction of knowing that the other Sheffield team had been relegated to the third tier

That first leg at Forest was a tight game ending in a 1-1 draw with Michael Brown scoring the Blades goal from the penalty spot and Michael Dawson getting sent off for Forest setting the tie up nicely for the second leg at Bramall Lane. The semi-final second leg game turned out to be one of the greatest games ever staged at the ground with another thirty thousand capacity crowd providing a bouncing atmosphere and the Blades deciding to skip the easy route and putting us fans through the whole range of emotions again.

The starting line-up that night was; *Kenny, Curtis, Jagielka, Page, Kozluk, Ndlovu, Brown, Rankine, Tonge, Windass and Asaba. Allison and Kab*ba were on the bench alongside *McCall, Montgomery and Peschisolido* with Warnock electing, as he often did, to have no reserve goalkeeper on the bench.

It was not the best of starts for the Blades and on the half hour mark United gifted Forest the lead when John Curtis attempted to clear a forward pass and slid the ball straight into the path of David Johnson who said '*Thank you very much*' and slammed the ball past Kenny from the edge of the box. Dean Windass got the crowd even more fired up than it already was as the Blades tried to get back into the game, banging his fists against the side of his head to show how hard he was after the Forest defenders had tried unsuccessfully to knock him about and the United fans rallied behind their team, but the score stayed at 1-0 as the half ended.

In the second half things got worse when on fifty eight minutes Mark Rankine switched off as Forest took a quick free kick in their own half and the move ended with Reid scoring a second for the Nottingham side and the Blades looked like they were going out in the semis yet again.

The Blades fans heads went down, but Warnock's side were not going to give up easily though and almost immediately earned a free kick on the edge of the box when Des Walker felled Asaba.

From the free kick Tonge tapped the ball to Brown and his low shot was deflected off Walker into the goal. Just eight minutes later a long ball from Kenny split the Forest defence and sub Kabba flicked the ball up in the air, like Paul Gascoigne had in Euro 96, to bemuse Des Walker before hammering in the equaliser. The roof nearly came off the kop as the Blades fans went wild at the equaliser, surely there would only be one winner now.

At ninety minutes the scores were still level at 2-2 and so it went into extra time and after the first period the scores remained the same. With the Blades now kicking towards the kop again we went for the win and six minutes into the second period of extra time another long clearance from Kenny found substitute Paul Peschisolido tight up against a defender. Pesky then turned the Forest defence inside out as he danced into the box and fired home a shot into the bottom corner of the net to put the Blades into the lead for the first time on the night. His dribble had been good, but it was nothing compared to the jinky run he did as he tore off his shirt and ran around the pitch in celebration as his team mates tried to catch him.

With just four minutes remaining Kabba outmuscled a defender and whipped in a cross which Des Walker could only turn into his own net with the keeper stranded and it looked like we were going to Cardiff. Walker, who had played for our city rivals, had not had the best of games and the crowd let him know it. Everyone in the ground must have thought that the game was won, but this was Sheffield United and they liked to keep us on the edge of our seats.

Forest went straight at the Blades and almost at once a shot from Huckerby could only be parried by Kenny and the ball bounced onto Robert Page who could only look on as it came off his legs and went into the net to make it 4-3. There then followed a tense three minutes of injury time with a lot of fingernails being bitten before the referee blew his whistle and the Blades fans could start to plan their trip to the Millennium Stadium. A few fans ran onto the pitch at the end and Warnock remonstrated with them to get off, but bloody hell Neil what do you expect?

With Wembley having been demolished to make way for a new stadium the play-off final was held at the Millennium Stadium in Cardiff and hordes of Blades made the journey down to South

Wales. I took Steve down in the car and after parking near Cardiff Castle we wandered around the city centre. Even before the game I got a bad feeling in my gut as the crowds of Blades fans seemed to be rather subdued in comparison with the gold shirted Wolves supporters who we had a mingle with. I don't know if it was the disappointment of two previous play-off failures or the semi-final defeats earlier in the year, but I got the impression that most fans were expecting disappointment again even before a ball had been kicked.

Credit to the staff at the Millennium Stadium the pre-match build-up was well organised and kept the fans entertained before the start of the game, which is more than the United team did when the match kicked off. The team by the way was; *Kenny, Curtis, Page, Jagielka, Kozluk, Ndlovu, Brown, Rankine, Tonge, Asaba and Kabba.* It was maybe a sign that Warnock had become cautious as there was a goalkeeper on the bench with *Gary Kelly* taking his place alongside *McCall, Montgomery, Peschisolido and Allison* and there had been a bit of a surprise when Windass did not even make the squad after putting in some fine performances towards the end of the season.

Once a ball actually had been kicked it did not take long for the fans fears to be realised. Wolves were all over the Blades and the team looked out of sorts from the start. Wolves were allowed to come onto us at will and Robert Page who had had a great season struggled to keep the Blades defence together. In a half where United struggled to get forward, Wolves made it look easy, going ahead after just six minutes when Kenny Miller collected a long ball and laid it off for Mark Kennedy to smash the ball into the net.

Worse was to come when on twenty two minutes a poorly defended corner was headed on by Paul Ince and United old boy Nathan Blake headed in to make it 2-0. The rout was complete just before the interval when Wolves ran the ball down the wing and crossed for Kenny Miller to head home the third. At half time it was 3-0 and we had not been in the game at all.

To make things worse, due to some strange quirk of the seating arrangements, I found myself sat in a block of Blades fans surrounded by blocks of Wolves fans on both sides. This meant that when we went onto the concourse at half time we were mixed in with loads of their fans who, as you might expect, were in a good frame of mind and giving some stick to the masses of Blades on the other side of a separating barrier. I had not been involved in any fighting at football for a few years but due to my rather disgruntled demeanour I am afraid that I found myself having to teach a couple of the more vociferous Wolves fans the error of their ways before the local constabulary stepped in to restore order. It turned out that I was not the only one losing my rag as we found out that Warnock had been shown a red card presumably for being Neil Warnock and would spend the second half in the stands.

The second half began with Warnock replacing Erskine with McCall and the Blades fans wondering why the Scott had not started the game. Almost from the off McCall bossed the midfield and the Blades started to take control of the game. Just three minutes into the second half an Ndlovu cross hit a Wolves defender and the referee gave what looked like a pretty soft penalty and we had a lifeline. Michael Brown placed the ball on the spot and we were all starting to think back to the comeback against Forest, but Brown who had been banging penalties home all season hit a poor shot at a perfect height for the keeper to save.

Peschisolido and Allison replaced Ndlovu and Kabba as the Blades tried to get back into the game. With Wolves now content to preserve their lead the Blades dominated play, but, with their keeper Murray putting in a man of the match performance a good effort from Pesky was saved and when Kennedy got away with blocking a shot on the line using his hand we knew it was not to be our day. This was confirmed when a brilliant free kick by Tonge hit the bar and Page put the rebound over the top. We had had the chances to turn the match around, but at the worst possible time our luck had deserted us.

Within seconds of the whistle going I was on my way back to the car as the Wolves fans celebrated promotion and the Blades fans, with heads down, set off on the long drive back home. Steve and I made the journey home with hardly a word spoken between us and were back home before nine p.m. feeling sick as parrots once more.

It had been a fantastic season with two cup semi-finals and a third place finish leading to a play-off final and was by far and away the best season we had had in well over ten years, but the nature of the way we went into that game against Wolves at first left me feeling as disappointed as I had been when suffering our various relegations. The thought did cross my mind that the team and tactics on that day had been set up in order for us to fail and I did wonder if somewhere within the Bramall Lane hierarchy it had been considered to be too soon to return to the top, but I just could not see Neil Warnock being any part of that sort of thinking. It was only some time later in that summer that I was able to start and put the season into perspective and start to feel happy about being a Blade again and looking forward to the next season.

2003/04

The 2003/04 season was entered into with a feeling of optimism. Once the disappointment of the final game of the previous season had faded most Blades fans reflected on what a great season it had actually been and were hoping to go one better this year.

We were now getting used to Neil Warnock's freshening up of the squad and the summer transfer window ended with Asaba, Windass and Yates plus a number of fringe players all moving out on free transfers and Simon Tracey retiring from the game having given the Blades some good service over the years. Coming in were defenders Andy Parkinson and Chris Armstrong for a combined half a million pounds plus, but the free signings of Chris Morgan, Jack Lester and Ashley Ward were what got most people talking. Paul Gerrard was also signed on loan to provide goalkeeping cover.

The season started slowly with two goalless draws before three wins had the fans believing their optimism had some substance. A 3-1 defeat at Forest, which I'm sure was of little consolation to their fans after the play-off loss, was quickly followed by two high scoring wins with the Blades thumping Toy Town (Rotherham United) 5-0 before beating Cardiff City 5-3. After going out of the League Cup to QPR, ending any hopes of another good cup run. We then won two away games at Bradford and Wimbledon which saw us sitting on top of the league after ten games, it was almost like 1971 all over again, just a division lower.

Typical of the Blades though being so high so soon must have given them a nosebleed and just like 1971 we lost our next match, this time at home to Sunderland and defeats at West Brom and

Millwall followed. A draw at Wigan was followed by a 2-1 loss to Reading at Bramall Lane and we were soon down to fourth place.

November proved to be a better month with just a solitary defeat at Ipswich interrupting a run of three wins and a draw and we were back up to third place with our promotion dreams still intact.

Eight points from a possible fifteen was not what we had hoped for in December but we were still in third place, although leaders Norwich seemed to be breaking away in the top spot. A Boxing Day win at Coventry however seemed like a good omen to me (clutching at straws again). A bad omen soon followed in the January transfer window when Michael Brown was sold to Tottenham. Brown had been fantastic for us the previous season scoring sixteen league goals as we finished in third place and, although he had only managed two goals this season, his partnership with Michael Tonge had to be one of the best in our division. He could be frustrating at times, diving about to win free kicks and trying to referee the game himself often turned officials against him, but he had been the engine of our side and would be missed. Peschisolido was also released and although Warnock brought in Simon Francis, Alan Wright, Paul Shaw and Andy Gray the squad just seemed to look a little weaker to me.

In the New Year Cardiff City were dispatched on their own turf in the third round of the FA Cup before another FA Cup win, 3-0 away at Nottingham Forest set us off on our latest cup journey. In between we had taken four points from two league games which had put us into third place with a game in hand over the top two. It was looking like developing into a season as good as the previous one, but, yet again the Blades baulked at the chance to push on and three successive defeats at Derby, Norwich and at home to Palace saw us suddenly standing ten points off the top and we were probably looking at another play-off competition if we were to get out of the division this time.

Two wins and two defeats in the next four games was not the best of returns and when Sunderland put us out of the cup in a quarter-final tie at their ground it left us with just the league to concentrate on once more.

It is always debated whether progressing in the cup competitions is a good thing or a bad thing in terms of a team's chances in the league. On the down side there are the chances of injuries or the dream of cup glory distracting players from the less glamorous league games. On the plus side winning can become a habit and cup victories, particularly against higher division opponents can add that vital ingredient, confidence. I am not sure if either case applies consistently but, while last season's cup runs had seemed to inspire the team to press on in the league, this year it seemed to be our exit that led to a bit of form with three wins and two draws following our exit from the cup. This left us in third place, albeit seven points behind the top two, with eight games to go. We had gone five games unbeaten at this point, all we needed was to remain consistent and we would be in the play-offs again.

Consistent we were and, in a typical Blades reaction to the chance of success, three defeats in a row to Cardiff, Forest and Sunderland saw us drop out of the play-off spots for the first time all season. It was very tight at the top end of the table though and a 2-1 win over Wimbledon saw us move back into the play-off spots before a shock 1-0 loss to Stoke at Bramall Lane saw us down in seventh place again. It was a case of hopes being raised one week with those hopes then dashed the next and although we won the next match away at Walsall we actually dropped to eighth place because Palace had played and won their game in hand. With just two games left we were a point off the play off places with us on sixty nine points and the three teams immediately above us on seventy. Two wins were called for to give us a chance. With our next game being at home to fourth placed Ipswich, just two points ahead of us, we had a real chance to take it to the last game of the season.

Typical of the Blades, once again when faced with the chance of glory we managed to blow it and a 1-1 draw saw us with just one away game left and a mountain to climb. We had played on a Friday night and so West Ham, Wigan and Palace, who were all above us, had a game in hand to play the following day and with them all having a better goal difference we now knew that it might not even get to that last game at Preston.

The next day West Ham and Palace both won but Wigan lost at Forest so we went into the last match of the season still with a slim hope of making the play-offs with us needing to win and hoping Ipswich and/or Palace lost and Wigan could get no more than a point in their game with West Ham. As we were also behind on goal difference three or four goals would also go down well.

In the end we did manage to score three goals that day, unfortunately so did Preston. With Ipswich and Wigan both drawing we ended up in eighth position, two points behind sixth place Palace who had lost their last game. I was left thinking that if we had just not conceded those three goals at Preston we would have made it on goal difference, but as my grandma used to say say *'If ifs and buts were sweets and nuts, we'd all have a merry Christmas.'*

2004/05

The 2004/5 season came with the good news that we were no longer in the First Division, the bad news was that we were still in the second tier of English football. There had been another re-branding and so we were now to be playing in what was called The Championship. It sounded quite grand but it was really only window dressing. Confusingly the third tier was now called League One and the bottom Division was now League Two. Anyone looking at a snapshot of statistics could be forgiven for thinking that every team had gained promotion.

Following our fade away at the end of the previous season Warnock embarked on another revamp of the squad and the departures of Page, Parkinson, Ndlovu, and Allison left gaps to be filled. Paul Thirwell, Jon Harley, and Andy Liddle were brought in but the biggest talking point was when Warnock went shopping at Hillsborough and brought in Leigh Bromby and Alan Quinn from our local rivals. In total the value of all these comings and goings was precisely nothing with all the movement being on free transfers.

It was an unfamiliar looking Blades team that kicked off the season but after three wins and two draws in the first six games we were in sixth place and it looked like being another season where we were going to be challenging at the right end of the table. By now you should be starting to be able to predict what happened next and, as you may have guessed, United lost the next three games at home to West Ham and away to Leicester and Wigan. We had dropped ten places to sixteenth and were now just five points clear of the drop zone. The Blades then put together an unbeaten run with the next seven games producing four draws and three wins and in this rollercoaster season there we were back in sixth place and play-off contenders again.

One of the other contenders was Ipswich Town and our next game was at Portman Road where a win and a favourable wind with the days other fixtures could see us move into third place. Instead we lost 5-1 and dropped out of the play-off places. This was a Neil Warnock team though and rather than feeling sorry for themselves the Blades reaction to the drubbing at Ipswich was to put together a nine match unbeaten run which saw us end the year in fifth place, just four points off the automatic promotion places.

January saw us progress in the FA Cup, with a 3-1 win over Premier League Aston Villa, and bring in Danny Cullip, Luke Beckett and another ex-Hillsborough boy in Derek Geary. In the opposite direction Warnock said goodbye to Jack Lester and sent several players out on loan, including a young lad called Billy Sharp who was the younger brother of a friend of my son Steve. Steve had had many kick abouts with Billy when he was younger and reckoned he was a very good player. Sharp had played just nine minutes for the Blades first team in two substitute appearances. He went on to score nine goals in sixteen appearances for Rushden and Diamonds and as the season went on many Blades fans had one eye on his performances for the Northamptonshire club as the Blades regularly stuttered in front of goal.

We managed to lose three of our four Championship games in January, but still went into February in fifth place. In a month that saw just three league games played, due to FA cup ties against West Ham and Arsenal both going to replays, the Blades picked up four points from a possible nine and headed into March down in eighth place but with games in hand.

Two wins, two defeats and a draw was a pretty average return from the five games played in March but in a tight division we were still in sixth place going into the sharp end of the season, so with eight games left and the automatic promotion places pretty much out of reach already it was the play-offs that were once again our target. I must admit that the introduction of the play-off system had been a success and we were now seeing the Blades still in contention for promotion right up until the end of the season on a regular basis. If the play-offs had not been introduced our season would have probably ended by March and the fans would have been watching meaningless games for weeks on end.

As it was we had eight games in which to try and gather enough points to extend our season and have a shot at glory once more. The first four of those games produced two wins and two draws including a 4-0 thumping of Leeds United at Elland Road. With four games left we were in seventh position just a point behind fifth placed Derby County who were our next opponents at Bramall Lane.

In a tense atmosphere for the crucial game against Derby the first half saw an energetic Rams side getting on top with Tommy Smith causing United problems and coming close with two shots from around the edge of the box, while the Blades could not manage to get a shot on target. The second half continued in a similar fashion and on seventy five minutes Peschisolido, who was now playing for Derby, broke through the Blades defence and Kenny had to come rushing out of the penalty area to block with his legs. Unfortunately the ball broke to Bisgaard who slotted home from eighteen yards as the Blades defenders tried to cover the empty goal.

This was a signal for the Blades to step it up in the final fifteen minutes and a cross/shot from Harley was tipped over the bar. From the resulting corner Bromby headed over and as the Blades pinned Derby back looking for an equaliser the best chance fell to Alan Quinn who managed to miss hit his shot which went embarrassingly wide for a throw in. I suppose that's what you get when you go shopping at Hillsborough! With that last chance missed Derby managed to hang on to their lead for a 1-0 win and our play-off chances became a little slimmer.

A 0-0 draw at Watford did not help improve those chances and when we lost the next match 1-0 at home to Millwall our inferior goal difference to the two teams who were three points above us effectively meant that another season was over. This meant the 4-2 defeat on the last day at Wolves was irrelevant and left us in eighth place for a second season running.

While our final position was a little disappointing, the Blades had kept the season alive almost until the end and it was probably the lack of goals that made the difference with just fifty seven goals scored. Andy Gray had top scored with fifteen of those goals but in a season where the likes of Ward, Kabba, Webber, Shaw, Cadermartari, Lester and Forte were all used as attacking options a productive partnership that might have turned some of our thirteen draws into wins could not be found.

2005/06

I did not look forward to the 2005/06 season with any real hope of success. Another upper mid-table finish, with possibly an outside chance of a play-off spot, given the rub of the green and a couple of regular goal scorers, was the height of my expectations. Mr Warnock must have had greater ambitions though as he decided that he needed to replace half the team and so he made Danny Webbers loan deal into a permanent transfer and brought in Neil Shipperly, Paul Ifill, Craig Short, David Unsworth and Keith Gillespie.

To make way for the new influx out went Andy Gray, Danny Cullip, Jon Harley, Paul Thirwell, and Andy Liddle. Ashley Ward and Stuart McCall retired but the biggest surprise for me and a lot of other Blades was that, after doing so well in his loan spell at Rushden and Diamonds, young Billy Sharp was not given a chance in the first team and was instead sold to Scunthorpe for one hundred and thirty five thousand pounds. It may have been that I was biased towards Billy as he was so well known to my son but I would have liked to have seen the local lad given his chance.

It was a different looking team and I didn't really know what to expect from them but I was soon changing my views on where we might finish as the Blades stormed into the new season. A 4-1 opening day win over Leicester gave a signal of our intentions and we went on to win ten of our first eleven games with the only defeat coming at QPR with a 2-1 reverse. After those eleven games we had thirty points and were seven points clear at the top of the Championship.

All good runs have to come to an end and we lost our twelfth game to Reading who also knocked us out of the League Cup and were to become a bit of a bogey side to us for a short time. This defeat did not knock us back too far though and another unbeaten run followed with eight matches coming without a loss. 4-0 wins away at Millwall and at home to Luton Town were the highlights of this run. In most seasons we would have been standing well clear at the top of the table, but Reading were having an even better time than us and had gone nineteen games unbeaten since losing on the opening day of the season and after twenty games they were one place and one point above us.

Our next game saw us lose 4-2 to Leicester at Filbert Street, but a 1-0 win over the old enemy at Bramall Lane followed by a 3-0 home victory over Burnley and a scoreless draw at Preston saw us go into the Christmas fixtures in second place, fourteen points clear of our nearest rivals. Now by this time I had a bit of history of following the Blades under my belt and so, even with the table looking as healthy as it did, I was not counting my chickens. I had seen the Blades at the top at Christmas and blow it before. I suppose my, and other Blades fans, scepticism is a bit of an insurance policy. If we did blow it we could say we knew it would happen, tempering our disappointment. If we went on to succeed, having expected failure, then we would be even more delighted.

A 3-1 home defeat to Norwich on Boxing day had the nerves jangling a little, but two days later a 1-0 win at Southampton was followed by victories over Stoke at home (2-1) and Hull away (3-1) giving us nine points from a possible twelve over the festive period. Annoyingly in the best season we had had for many years Reading had extended their unbeaten run to an amazing twenty seven games and stood ten points clear of us at the top with Leeds United now eight points behind us in third place.

Our next game was an FA Cup tie at home to Colchester United who were going well in League One. I don't know if professional football clubs would ever 'throw' cup games to concentrate on the league, but I am sure that some sides who had a shot at promotion may have put 'less emphasis' on some of the knockout competitions from time to time. I will always prefer to believe that we had our minds on our league campaign when we played this game as the alternative is to have to accept that we lost the game 2-1 to lower league opposition fair and square.

The January transfer window saw the recruitment of Ade Akinbiyi, Chris Luketti, Bruce Dyer, Gary Flitcroft and Geoff Horsfield, although Horsfield spent most of the rest of the season out on loan. The Blades had also seen the return of Brian Deane for his third spell at the Lane but this move seemed to be more of a gesture to the fans than having any real intent to play the Blades hero on a regular basis

Now with only the promotion charge to worry about the Blades could set about the New Year's fixtures with determination and focus. With two wins, two draws and a shock 4-1 home loss to Watford I am not too sure what it was we were focusing on and with the next match being at home to runaway leaders Reading we needed to get it together sharpish. We were now twelve points behind them and anything other than a win would probably be conceding the title to the Berkshire club.

The Reading game was on a Tuesday night and I had managed to wangle a seat in the Directors Box complete with three course meal before the match and all the other trimmings that go with mixing in such esteemed company. Before the game I had asked one of the other directors whether the board meetings were more colourful with Sean Bean being a director at the time. I will not break the confidentiality that I agreed to by repeating his answer, but from what he told me it did seem that the actor had on occasions brought a little of the terraces to the table.

Speaking of the actor he was sat directly behind me throughout the game and he definitely brought colour to the plush seats in the posh part of the South Stand that night. As far as I could see he was the only one in my immediate surroundings that was not wearing a collar and tie and his language throughout the game (mostly aimed at Dave Kitson who was putting himself about, not always fairly) was almost making me blush, and that takes some doing.

At half time I went into the director's suite for the customary bowl of soup and found myself standing next to David O'Leary who was Aston Villa manager at the time and was rumoured to be interested in Phil Jagielka. As I was stood there my mobile phone rang and our Steve asked me how the game was going. While talking to Steve I mentioned that I was stood close to O'Leary and Steve, with his usual wit said 'Ask him what's going on with that nose of his.' referring to the former Arsenal man's snout like proboscis. It should go without saying that I did not ask.

With a minute to go, in a game that we had deserved to win, we were being held at 1-1 by a Reading side that had been lucky to hang on to their unbeaten run. Then the referee awarded Reading a penalty. Paddy Kenny had made a terrific save at the feet of a Reading striker and as both players scrambled to get up they came together and the referee decided that was enough for a spot kick. The crowd was furious, none more so than Sean Bean who left his seat and ran down to the front of the stand ranting at the ref and being restrained by stewards as he tried to get at the official. Definitely not the behaviour you would expect of a director!

With the penalty award seeming harsh the football gods stepped in, seeing to it that Paddy Kenny saved Dave Kitson's spot kick and the match ended in a draw which probably saw our title aspirations gone.

The next game was at Hillsborough and, whatever our position in the league, this is a game that we go into looking for the win. A good start saw the Blades go ahead when a brilliant free kick from Tonge was whipped into the far side of the goal and Tonge made the top corner sign to his team mates and the home fans looking down from the kop. United dominated and increased their lead when Akinbiyi lashed a shot home with virtually the last kick of the first half. The Blades could have gone further ahead, but Akinbiyi could only head Bruce Dyer's cross over the bar when it looked easier to score. They came back at us but it took a devious trick to get them back into the game when Chris Brunt threw a leg at Chris Morgan and went over in the box fooling the ref into giving a penalty. This time Kenny could not make the save and despite a late charge by our neighbours we hung on for a 2-1 win and another Sheffield double whammy.

This should have been the spur to push us on with our promotion charge but instead we gained just one point from the next four games and with Reading now sixteen points clear at the top and virtually assured of the title we were now starting to look nervously over our shoulders at Leeds who were now just four points behind with a game in hand and we still had them to play at Bramall Lane..

A 3-0 home win over Southampton was followed by a point at Stoke which set us up for a vital game at home to Hull City. With Leeds and Watford both having lost their last games and fallen seven points behind us with just five games to go a win would edge us to within touching distance of promotion.

The Blades started the game well but missed some good chances before a cross from Tonge out on the right wing found Shipperley who stooped to head in the opener and saw us going

112

into half time with a 1-0 lead. In the second half Danny Webber broke down the left and put in a superb cross which Paul Ifill headed in at the near post and it looked like the victory was ours.

Hull were not to be written off though and some terrible defending allowed Elliott in to make it 2-1. Then it looked as though we had hit the self-destruct button. Kenny looked like he had given away a penalty when he appeared to have grabbed a Hull player around the ankle, but the referee somehow did not see it. Minutes later Hull levelled when more poor defending allowed them in for a second and then Kenny was injured saving at the feet of an Hull striker as they pressed for a winner. Kenny stayed on the pitch but was soon in the wars again when he collided with skipper Chris Morgan and was left looking dazed and confused, but then again that was probably his normal look most weeks.

With the keeper hobbling around not knowing what day it was and with no sub available the best way for the Blades to protect him was to attack the Hull goal and that is what they did, with Kabba coming closest to scoring. Then with what could be only seconds to go there was a scramble in the box and David Unsworth, of all people, popped up to stick the bobbling ball into the net for a 3-2 victory. The whistle went and the crowd went wild with most of the Blades fans in the ground giving a resounding chorus of '*That's why we're going up….. That's why we're going up,*' as the players took the applause.

Leeds United were now nine points behind us with four games left and they were next up at Bramall Lane. Before that game though there was the matter of a Good Friday match at Cardiff. I would have loved to have gone to that game but having gotten the bug for exotic holidays I found myself in a five star hotel in India, so I had to keep up to date with the game by looking at the internet between cocktails. It's a hard life!

The result was a 1-0 win for the Blades with Danny Webber getting the decisive goal. We were now eleven points clear of third placed Watford with just three games left, but Leeds had four games to play and were due to play Reading at Elland Road the following day and a win would mean that they could still catch us. With Leeds to come next for us a win over Reading, who by now had been crowned champions and had nothing but pride to play for, could have been a recipe for an end of season disaster. I was praying that the Berkshire outfit would prove just as frustrating for Leeds as they had for us.

There is a time difference of four and a half hours between England and India and I made a little bit of a mistake when doing my calculations and so when I logged on to the internet in the hotel lobby I found that the game at Elland Road was almost over and the score was 1-1. Although I had missed most of the game I was actually glad because, after finding out that Leeds had been winning, I was happy to have avoided the tension while I was on my holiday. It was around nine fifteen in the evening and everyone at the hotel, including me, was dressed up for the night-time entertainment. The hotel lobby was just beside the infinity pool and lots of guests were sat by the pool having drinks from the bar in the lobby. As the final whistle went, confirming that the Blades had been promoted to the Premier League after a twelve year absence, I rushed out of the lobby, cheering at the top of my voice, and dived headlong and fully clothed into the pool. Everyone around the pool must have wondered what the hell was going on, but my wife explained the situation to them as I took a complimentary golf buggy back to our villa to get some dry clothes.

I spent the rest of the holiday with a massive smile on my face and did not even tune in for the Leeds game, which we drew 1-1 or the away game at Luton that followed, and also ended 1-1. I did however make it back in time for the final game of the season against Crystal Palace where the game, a 1-0 win, was an irrelevance as the Blades fans and players just waited for the ninety minutes to tick away so that they could begin the celebrations. I do however remember that the fans spent a lot of the game taking the micky out of Palace keeper Gabor Kiraly singing '*Track suit from Matalan….Track suit from Matalan,*' in tribute to his long grey jogging bottoms.

The match also saw Craig Short coming off towards the end of the game to applause that marked the end of his playing career and with a couple of minutes to go Brian Deane was brought onto the pitch and he was warmly welcomed as he too made the last appearance of his career and was part of a Blades side promoted to the top flight for the second time. It was the end of a fabulous season that saw us finish with automatic promotion, nine points clear of third place. No one was really bothered at that point how we would cope, back in the big time the following season.

2006/07

The summer was spent preparing to play back in the big time. The squad obviously needed to be strengthened in order to cope with the demands of the Premier League and the quality of opposition we would be playing. What we needed were some experienced Premier League players. We weren't expecting Warnock to be raiding Man United or Arsenal's first team, but some top level quality needed to be added to the enthusiasm of the players who had got us up.

What we got was Claude Davis from Preston, an awkward looking, gangling centre half who, in my opinion, was not the best positional player and was to prove to have a propensity for leaving the ball to run through to opposition forwards rather than making a simple clearance. Even when he did get the ball away it always tended to look last ditch. As well as Davis we also signed Mikele Leigertwood from Palace, a competent midfielder but not necessarily Premiership class, and Christian Nade an unknown French striker, but I suppose we were going to be playing in the Premier League so we needed a foreigner. Colin Kazim Richards was signed from League One Brighton and although he actually turned out to be quite a good player we were not filled with confidence when we heard Warnock had been shopping in the lower rather than higher divisions. The one decent looking signing, although still not from the top flight, was Rob Hulse from Leeds. We actually took one of their best players for a change.

Out of the squad went Simon Francis, Bruce Dyer and Luke Beckett. It looked like a good Championship squad, but we were not in the Championship any longer and it looked like Warnock's team's enthusiasm and battling qualities were going to be needed again if we were to stand a chance of staying up. As the season approached no one had any doubts that this was going to be a battle for survival.

The first game back in the big time was against the previous season's FA Cup winners Liverpool at Bramall Lane. A full house saw the Blades put in a good shift and, after a goalless first half and some good work by Paddy Kenny, they were ecstatic when Rob Hulse got off the mark to put us in front. Liverpool clearly had the better players and put us under some pressure, but our spirit and desire kept the game tight. That is until the referee gave a penalty when he said that Chris Morgan had made contact with Gerrard in the box. Replays clearly showed that there had been no contact and later the referee changed his tune and said that he had given the kick because he believed there was intent to foul the Liverpool man. As you can imagine Neil Warnock had some choice words to say about the ref and the game ended in a 1-1 draw and was the first of many pieces of bad luck that were to plague the Blades in this season.

Defeats at Spurs and Fulham followed before the next home game against Blackburn, a game in which three penalties were given and saved (two to us and one to them) and the match ended scoreless. We were then beaten 2-1 at home to Reading, who really had become our bogey team, and 3-0 at Arsenal, to no one's surprise, leaving us rock bottom after six games.

The next game was at home to Middlesbrough and for this one I had got myself a spot in one of the executive boxes in the John Street stand courtesy of Westfield Health who did a lot of business with my employers at the time. I enjoyed the experience almost as much as the game. A first half goal by Rob Hulse (who was the only player to have scored for the Blades at that point) had been cancelled out by a Yakuba goal and we were facing another draw when a clearance by a 'Boro defender was taken on the chest by Jagielka about forty yards out and, reminiscent of his goal against Leeds four years earlier he came onto the bouncing ball and hit a shot into the far corner of the net securing United's first win back in the top flight and taking us out of the relegation zone.

The next game was away at Manchester City and I could not resist the opportunity to go and see their new stadium. City had been in there for a few years but as we had been in the division below this was my first chance to go and see it in person. From the outside it looked quite impressive with the circular ramps looking similar to the ones at the San Siro in Milan. The seats offered a good view and the pies were good, but my abiding memory was of disappointment with the lack of internal finishes and bare concrete everywhere. The game was also slightly disappointing as we came away with a 0-0 draw against a struggling City side that were there for the taking that day.

We then lost the next three games on the trot and were back in the last relegation place before a Danny Webber goal gave us our first away win in front of fifty thousand at St James's Park which eased us just out of the drop zone again. To be fair we had expected a relegation battle and that is exactly what we were getting. A 2-2 draw after being two down at home to Bolton, who were third in the table, didn't seem like a bad result but our next game was at home to Man United and we got what we expected and lost 2-1 after cheekily taking the lead. We were then away to West Ham and lost 1-0 when another poor decision by the officials ruled out what looked like a perfectly good equaliser and we were still in eighteenth place. (We did not know it at the time, but that decision could possibly have turned out to be one of the most costly in the Blades history.)

The Blades then dug deep and did what they had done many times under Warnock and responded to adversity with two wins over both of the teams below us and we were up to sixteenth place. A home draw with Villa slowed down progress before an away victory at Wigan lifted us to fourteenth place, our highest of the season. We then went into the Christmas period facing four games in just nine days and we managed to lose three of the four. The one we did not lose was a classic. We were at home to Arsenal on the thirtieth of December and thirty two thousand packed into Bramall Lane expecting us to be well beaten by the third placed club. Most Blades were surprised by the inclusion of Christian Nade in the starting line-up, as so far he had looked like the French second tier player that he was, but after a couple of half chances to the Blades and some solid defending the ball was passed forward to the Frenchman who spun away from Kolo Toure, who had gotten too tight, and ran on to slot past Lehman in the Arsenal net to register his first goal for the Blades. More drama was to come though as Kenny in United's goal injured his groin and could not continue. As was often the case with Warnock there was no keeper on the bench so Phil Jagielka had to put on the gloves for the last half hour and he put in a great performance including one save where he tipped over a Van-Persie effort that looked goal bound. The Blades managed to hang on for a famous victory that left us heading into the New Year in fifteenth spot.

The January transfer window saw Warnock bring in more players with Matt Kilgallon coming from Sunderland and John Stead coming in to offer something different up front alongside Hulse. Also coming in were two wastes of good money Ahmed Fathi and Luton Shelton. In the opposite direction went a good chunk of the promotion squad in Paul Ifill, Ade Akinbiyi, Steve Kabba and Neil Shipperley. The other player to go was David Unsworth in a move that was to come back and bite us later.

A 1-1- draw against Portsmouth was followed by a game at our bogey team Reading and it was another game that sticks in the mind for the wrong reasons. As well as losing the game 3-1 Keith Gillespie managed to get himself in the record books when he came on as substitute and elbowed Reading's Stephen Hunt in the face. The linesman flagged immediately and after some discussion with the referee Gillespie was sent off. In the usual rumpus that follows a red card Gillespie managed to chin Hunt again and then ex-Blade Wally Downes, the Reading coach, pushed Warnock and both Downes and Warnock were sent to the stand. As the play had not resumed since Gillespie had entered the field he was technically sent off after playing zero seconds.

Two wins and a draw were mixed in with three defeats in the next six games but the worst news was that in the last of those games Rob Hulse broke his leg while trying to beat the keeper to the ball at Chelsea and was out for the rest of the season. This was a massive blow as Hulse had looked a Premier League quality player and had managed to score eight goals in a side that had struggled to create chances against top tier opposition. We were now left with just Stead, Webber and Nade as attacking options and we were just one place above the drop zone, it was going to be close.

Things were not helped when we lost our next two games first at Bolton and then at home to Newcastle United. The following game therefore took on extra significance as it was at home to West Ham who were one place and two points behind us in nineteenth place in the table. A win was a must and Warnock's Blades responded with what was their best performance of the season beating the Hammers 3-0 and propelling us out of the relegation spots to sit between Charlton and Wigan in a still precarious seventeenth place with just five games left. Three of those games were against fellow relegation candidates Charlton, Watford and Wigan so we fancied our chances having done pretty well against the teams around us during the season. Unfortunately the first of the other two games was away to Manchester United and Wayne Rooney saw to it that, despite a good performance, we came away with no points from a 2-0 defeat.

Charlton away was next on the horizon and it was vital that we did not lose. After going behind, the Blades rallied and a Jon Stead goal gave us a point that kept us out of the relegation zone. We then faced a home game against Watford, who by now were already down, and in a game that was tighter than I would have liked a goal from a deflected Michael Tonge shot gave us a vital three points. We were now in fifteenth place but still only three points clear of the third relegation spot. Any points that we could pick up at Aston Villa the following week would go a long way towards securing the survival that was the only real target at the start of the season.

Aston Villa came around and in what Warnock admitted afterwards was probably a tactical error he sent out a team to go for the win rather than set up to keep tight and hope for a point or maybe even a breakaway winner. The game was a late afternoon kick off and with West Ham and Fulham having already won it was even more important that we did not lose, but the team seemed to struggle with the pressure they were under and lost the game 3-0 in what was probably one of their worst performances when they needed one of their best. Warnock was venting his spleen again when he heard that Liverpool had played a weakened team against Fulham, resting players in preparation for a Champions League final and allowing the London club to take an unlikely three precious points. He may have had a point but sometimes I wished he would have just shut up and concentrated on our games. Despite the results we were still in sixteenth place, three points clear of eighteenth placed Wigan and above West Ham on goal difference. A point at home against Wigan on the last day of the season would see us safe, as would West Ham losing at Manchester United regardless of our result.

I was pretty confident that we would stay up. I did not think we would lose to Wigan in front of a packed house at Bramall Lane nor did I believe West Ham would get anything but a defeat at

Man United as I jetted off on another ill-timed holiday, this time to a small island just off the coast of Mexico. The place I stayed in was lovely but had poor TV reception and so on the final day of the season I sat by a television that had reasonable sound, but a picture that looked more like a snowstorm in the Arctic. There was no live coverage of our game available so the best I could do was listen to the commentary on TV as somewhere beneath the snow Manchester United were playing West Ham.

The whole relegation battle had already been heated up when Carlos Tevez's transfer to West Ham had been investigated and although his registration had been deemed to be outside the rules, to most football fans bemusement, the Hammers had not been given a points deduction. At any other level of football if a team fields a player that is not correctly registered then points are deducted every time, in this case the authorities decided not to do so. Nevertheless we went into the last match with our destiny in our own hands.

As I listened to the game being played in Manchester the sound kept coming and going, but as the commentators kept everyone updated with the other important games as well as the one they were watching the twists and turns started to unfold. The Blades conceded an early goal against Wigan and our position started to look dodgy but with West Ham at 0-0 we were still ok. Then we equalised which put us safe again, but almost at the same time the unthinkable happened, West Ham took the lead at Old Trafford and just to rub salt into the wound it was Tevez that got the goal.

We were now only one place above safety and a goal from Wigan would send us down on goal difference. With that thought in my head the next news from Bramall Lane was the last thing I wanted to hear. Wigan had been awarded a penalty and when David Unsworth, who we had sold to Wigan in January, scored we were going down. Even then with the seconds ticking away there was still time for Danny Webber to break through the Wigan defence and chip the keeper. The crowd at Bramall Lane held their breath and, listening to the report on the incident thousands of miles away, I nearly had an heart attack as Webber's shot hit the inside of the post and bounced away to safety and with that last chance we were sent back down to the Championship, in controversial circumstances once more, after just one season back at the top.

I was on a Caribbean island soaking up the sun and enjoying twenty four hour all-inclusive facilities, but I felt anything but in the holiday mood. Just to make matters worse there was a party of Londoners, who were mostly West Ham fans, at the hotel for a wedding and so for the rest of the day and a couple of days afterwards I had to watch around forty of them all celebrating their escape as I sulked into my mojitos, The contract to the previous year's holiday couldn't have been greater.

In the subsequent weeks legal proceedings and appeals to the FA about the Tevez saga failed to see West Ham deducted the points that everyone knew should have happened and our last hope of avoiding relegation was gone. It was no real surprise that the FA did not do their job as with West Ham legend Trevor Brooking and ex Hillsborough chairman Dave Richards high up in the FA hierarchy a decision in favour of the Blades was never going to be the outcome. Afterwards United looked to sue West Ham and the London club eventually settled out of court paying a multi-million pound sum to the Blades which is of little compensation to the fans but a very good indicator of who should really have gone down.

To make matters worse after the Wigan game it was reported that Sean Bean had aimed a foul mouthed tirade at Neil Warnock in front of his family (a report that Bean has denied) and Warnock decided that enough was enough and resigned. Having previously seen Mr Bean in action I know which version I am personally inclined to believe, but whatever actually happened the outcome was that probably the best qualified man to lead us on a promotion charge the following season was gone and the next few years would come to show what a mistake it was to let Warnock go that day.

We had been relegated by the narrowest of margins, just one goal, but the truth was that even if we had survived we were a team punching above its weight and without substantial investment would have probably struggled again the following year.

The Warnock years were over and he has to go down as one of the Blades best managers. He was a promotion expert but we will never know if he would have been able to make it in the top flight over a sustained period of time. It had been an interesting ride but now we were back to riding in the Championship once more.

One Step Forward, Two Steps Back

2007/08

With Warnock gone we needed a new manager and we got one in the shape of Bryan Robson. On the face of it this seemed like a good appointment. The former England captain had had a reasonably successful spell at Middlesbrough where he had guided them to two promotions, one relegation and three losing appearances at Wembley. He had also guided West Brom to safety in the Premier League against very heavy odds so he seemed like a good fit for the Blades. He was also a figure that was generally respected by the football authorities which was a sharp contrast to Neil Warnock. Robson had however had a less successful spell as manager of Bradford City where the resources were a little more sparse, so only time would tell how he would fare at Bramall Lane.

Robson would want to play his own style of football and the Blades were not going to be getting Premier League income so transfer business was busy with Jagielka, Kazim-Richards, Davis, Leigertwood, Fathi and Nade all being sold to finance new arrivals James Beattie, Gary Naysmith, David Carney and Lee Hendrie and to bring back Billy Sharp from Scunthorpe as well as put a few million back into United's coffers.

I am not sure if Robson wanted to bring Sharp back to the Lane, but there had been quite a lot of talk amongst the fans of his scoring exploits at Scunthorpe while we had been struggling to get the goals the previous season and I think it was more of a stunt on Robson's part to try and get the fans onside, and sell a few season tickets, as it became clear as the season got underway that Billy was not going to be played in his best position as a main striker and he was often to be seen labouring out wide in more of an attacking midfield role. During the first half of the season Robson also brought in loan players Phil Bardsley from Man United and Gary Cahill from Aston Villa to bolster the defence.

So the 2007/08 season got underway with a new look to the team and a stark contrast in the opposition. Where twelve months earlier we were welcoming a star studded Liverpool side, we were now playing hosts to Colchester United on the first day. The result however was not much different with a 2-2 draw being somewhat less than we had hoped for.

More uninspiring results followed and after ten games we had only managed to win two and stood in twenty first place, just one point clear of the drop zone. We were managing to score goals most weeks but we were also conceding too many with sixteen scored but nineteen conceded in those first ten games. It was already starting to look like Robson was reproducing the form he had shown at Bradford rather than that of his time at Middlesbrough. Any hopes of a first time return to the Premier League seemed to have evaporated and we were only just going into October! The fans were getting restless and there were many rumours going around that Robson had a drinking problem. With the results the Blades were getting I am sure many of the fans were turning to the bottle too.

The next nine games saw five wins and three draws with just a solitary defeat at home to Plymouth and while the goals were not coming as quickly, with the Blades only scoring a single goal in five of those games, we had tightened up at the back and had only conceded four goals in that nine game spell. We had also managed to climb back up to eleventh place and were amazingly only three points off the play-off spots.

December was going to be a big month but although we managed a 1-0 win over local rivals Barnsley that was the only win in Robson's next six games with four defeats and a 1-1 draw at home to Blackpool on Boxing Day it had been a bad month and we went into 2008 in sixteenth place.

With the season already looking like a write-off ex Hillsborough pair Leigh Bromby and Alan Quinn were sold to bring in a bit of money and Robson had to rely on loans bringing in thirty eight year old Gary Speed from Bolton along with Lee Martin and David Cotterill and signing thirty five year old Ugo Ehiogu on a free transfer from Glasgow Rangers. My heart did not exactly start racing in anticipation of a surge up the table. The loan system was also used to help with the wage bill for the large squad with fifteen players being loaned out in January.

FA Cup wins over Bolton and Manchester City could not disguise the fact that we were struggling in the league. With wins rarer than rocking horse shit we were going nowhere fast. After starting the New Year with just a single victory over QPR sitting among a defeat at out nearest neighbours and five draws, three of which were scoreless, the board called time on Robson's reign as the fans discontent began to be voiced ever louder. With the Blades in a lowly sixteenth position it was time for another manager to have a go and Neil Warnock's former assistant Kevin Blackwell was appointed as successor to Robson.

Blackwell did not make an immediate impact with a fifth round FA Cup exit in a replayed tie at Middlesbrough being surrounded by a 1-1 draw at QPR and a 2-0 home defeat to play-off contenders Charlton. Blackwell was however slowly starting to turn things around and after a 1-1 draw at Ipswich the Blades won four on the bounce to lift us up to twelfth place and start to bring back some confidence to the team. A 3-1 defeat at Preston was just a slight bump in the road to recovery and the Blades went on to win four of the next five games with the only points dropped being, predictably, in a 2-2 draw with Sheffield's other lot at Bramall Lane.

We now had just one game left in the season and incredibly we were just two points off the play-off spots. If we won our last match at Southampton and other results went our way there was still a possibility that we could sneak into the play-offs at the last minute. Southampton for their part were in the third relegation place and were desperate for a win, and other results to go their way, to try and avoid the drop. This was Sheffield United however and when several results are required for a particular outcome they only ever conspire to happen to put us down rather than up and so, predictably for anyone who has followed the Blades for any time, the teams above us gained the points they needed and we lost 3-2 at St Marys where Southampton had the last day luck that we never seemed to get in a relegation battle and saw Leicester drawing 0-0 at Stoke to save the Saints and relegate the Foxes instead.

The season ended with the Blades in ninth place and me and many other fans wondering what might have happened if Robson had been sacked at Christmas rather than on Valentine's Day. Well maybe next season would bring the answer.

2008/09

The failure to secure an immediate return to the top tier meant that costs needed to be looked at and income was raised from the sale of Rob Hulse, who was now fit again, but nowhere near the player he had been before his injury, and our best player over the last few seasons Michael Tonge. James Beattie was heavily rumoured to be going too, but come the end of the window he was still there. Armstrong, Stead and Shelton also brought in a few quid, some of which was given to Blackwell to spend.

Darius Henderson was brought in along with David Cotterill and with the fees for those two taking up all of the money made available, free transfers in the shape of Gary Speed, who had been on loan the previous season, and Jihai Sun along with loan players Greg Halford, Nathan Dyer and Brian Howard concluded the business for the summer transfer window.

The 2008/09 season started with a 1-0 defeat away to Championship favourites Birmingham with Kevin Phillips breaking Blades fans hearts with a ninety third minute winner, but the fans were given a boost in the first home league game when local lad and crowd favourite Billy Sharp scored a hat trick in a 3-0 win over QPR. It was a rare glimpse of what Billy was capable of when allowed to play his own game. Unfortunately with James Beattie and the completely different style of Darius Henderson to accommodate, Sharp did not really get enough opportunities to show what he could do consistently in front of goal. Beattie was clearly a good striker and I am sure he must have been on good wages so it was pretty obvious he was going to get the main striker role when fit. Sharp got quite a few starts and was credited with a few good assists but was often to be found running the channels while Beattie ploughed the furrow down the middle. It would have been interesting to see how it would have panned out if Billy had got the chance to play in between the posts in this spell at the Lane.

That win over QPR was followed up by a 3-1 victory at Blackpool and then an awkward little spell where we could only draw our two home games and lose two games on our travels. This left us in an uninspiring fifteenth place after seven games and the season looked like being much like the last. After a 6-0 League Cup defeat by what was basically an Arsenal youth team the Blades seemed to have been given the wakeup call they needed and they won the next three on the bounce to lift us up to fourth in the table and our season was underway.

After losing in our next game to the old enemy at Hillsborough, in a game where Kilgallon was sent off, we strung together a five game unbeaten run cumulating in a 2-1 away win at Barnsley where James Beattie annoyed me with his greediness. The Blades had broken away and Beattie was on the ball in a wide right position, Two Blades players had burst forward in support and were unmarked as they reached the penalty area. Any sort of ball played across the box would have left a tap in for a certain goal, but Beattie quite deliberately took the ball to the by-line and played the ball off the Barnsley defenders legs for a corner. He would then be able to get in the middle and have a chance of scoring from the corner. It seemed to me like James Beattie was more interested in promoting his own stats than those of the team.

The next game was at home to bogey side Reading and we lost 2-0 in another game where we played pretty well but did not get the result. A good reaction to that loss resulted in a 5-2 away win at Charlton and in an up and down period we lost at home to Wolves and Burnley but picked up away draws at Ipswich and Swansea along with a win at Forest. The away form was definitely carrying us at this point. Two Draws and a win over Christmas took us into the New Year and a 1-0 win over Norwich saw us in a fourth place play-off position going into the second half of the season. The top three of Wolves, Reading and Birmingham seemed to be breaking away but there were still twenty games to go and, as we have seen before, anything can happen.

The January transfer window saw top scorer James Beattie sold to Stoke and Gillespie and Fortune given free transfers while Brian Howard's loan was made into a permanent transfer, Jamie Ward cane in from League Two Chesterfield and Leigh Bromby came back from Watford. To fill the hole left up front two donkeys were brought in on loan in the shape of Craig Beattie and Anthony Stokes.

Two FA Cup wins and a league victory at Watford saw the good run continuing but then a surprise home loss to Doncaster checked progress. A 2-1 away win at Southampton was balanced by a 2-1 loss to the blue and white mob, which could have been a real setback to our season but instead inspired the Blades to go on an eleven match unbeaten run which saw us come out of the Easter fixtures in third place, just one point off the automatic promotion places with just three games to go. We had even managed to get a 1-0 win away at bogey side Reading along the way.

The next game was away to Burnley and a win would have really turned the pressure up on Birmingham. At this stage the Blades had gone a club record fifteen away games without defeat but we ended up losing 1-0 while the Brummies won 1-0 at Watford meaning the pressure was now on us. A young full back called Kyle Walker was promoted to the first team and first impressions were that he might just make a very good player. He had blistering pace and was capable of a good delivery into the box. Time would tell what was to become of him.

We were four points behind and looking at the play-offs again, but a win over Swansea in the next game and Birmingham surprisingly loosing at home to Preston meant that we went into the last game away to Crystal Palace still with an outside chance of automatic promotion. Neil Warnock was manager at Palace and there was some talk of whether, as a keen Blades fan, he might not motivate his side as much as he usually would to give the Blades an easier ride. Warnock though would never send a side out with anything other than a win in mind and was probably still smarting from the events following the Wigan disaster and his side battled well. Goalkeeper Spironi in particular made two brilliant saves to deny Jamie Ward and the referee did not help our cause turning down two good penalty appeals, both after fouls on Henderson. When Morgan then hit the post late on we knew it was not our day. As it turned out Birmingham's last day win at Reading meant that our 0-0 draw at Selhurst Park was of no significance and we finished in third spot. A play-off semi-final against Preston was now standing between us and another appearance at Wembley.

Due to our third placed finish the first leg was away from home and Preston put us under some pressure at their place. They took the lead through St Ledger and also hit the post, but early in the second half Brian Howard equalised and the Blades could have wrapped it up in that first game if the Beattie playing up front had been James and not Craig. Twice he was clean through and after a poor effort the first time he then chose to keep the ball and waste the chance when a simple square ball would have left a tap in from supporting players. As it was we had to settle for a 1-1 draw and home advantage in the second leg.

Injuries were taking their toll and both Henderson and Ward were not fit for the second leg leaving us looking very light up front. The Blades excepted good pressure on Preston in the first half in a feisty game, where fat lad Parkin was lucky not to get a red card when he put his studs through Greg Halfords belly, but the lack of quality up front was apparent. In the second half more pressure was applied and then Kyle Walker burst down the right and whipped in a peach of a cross which Halford rose to glance in to the net for the lead. The fat bloke up front for Preston was still throwing his weight about and forced a save from Kenny and then Craig Beattie found himself through on goal again but predictably managed to waste the chance. Nevertheless the one goal that we had managed to score was enough to see us through to a play-off final at the new Wembley Stadium.

I decided to go big on this one so I procured tickets for the Club Wembley seats and I can report that the seats, view and hospitality on offer were excellent. I can also report that the game was not. Our opponents were Burnley and the omens were not good, having lost to them twice already that season, but we had played well in both matches and had been unlucky not to get anything from the two games so all was not lost. That is until the game kicked off. Yet again we seemed to have saved our worst performance for the most important game and while we put ourselves about it was Burnley who dominated the play and opened the scoring with a fine effort from Wade Elliott. The Blades best opportunity of the first half was when Brian Howard seemed to have been brought down in the box. Referee Mike Dean, who never seemed to give the Blades anything, declined to give a penalty.

In the second half Burnley continued to dominate and Montgomery was forced to clear off the line to deny Burnley a second. Walker also made a brilliant challenge, using his pace to get across Blake when he seemed certain to score and Naughton also had to block another good effort. Again United's only real opportunity was when Walker was brought down as he burst into the box but Mr Dean was giving us nothing that day. Now I say nothing, but what he did decide to give us was a red card when substitute Jamie Ward handled the ball twice in quick succession and with that our chances of promotion were gone.

The record books show the score as being 1-0 but in reality the game was much more one sided than that and we were lucky not to have lost three or four nil on the day. I drove home, yet again, sick as a parrot as another big day out had come to nothing and, as fans of all play-off losers will tell you, a very good season ended with that awful feeling of disappointment that masks the achievements of the forty six games that preceded it. This had been our fifth attempt in the play-offs without success and while overall I think the system is a good thing for football in general, keeping alive the hopes of many clubs right until the end of the season, for me personally the heartache of getting so close so often and then being let down was taking its toll and I swore to myself I would not put myself through another play-off final. As far as I was concerned, at this moment in time, if we could not get automatic promotion I would rather the Blades finished seventh than lose in the play-offs again.

2009/10

Some teams, when they come so agonisingly close to success, build on what got them so close and push again to make the improvements that will get them to the next level. A couple of home draws turned into wins, an odd goal here and there or just a tiny piece of luck to change one game was all we were short of in our attempt to get back to the Premier League, so what did we do? Dismantle the squad that nearly got us there of course.

The two brightest sparks in the previous season were the emerging young full backs Kyle Naughton and Kyle Walker. Both were sold to Tottenham (although Walker was loaned back to us, supposedly for the season). Brian Howard was sold along with Leigh Bromby who had only recently returned and promising young striker Billy Sharp was loaned to Doncaster Rovers for the season where once again he showed that, played in the right position, he could score a goal every two games. Danny Webber was released, Ugo Ehiogu retired and a host of fringe players were let go leaving Blackwood with only around fourteen professionals on the books.

In came Ched Evans from Manchester City a promising young striker, but with little first team experience, Lee Williamson from Watford, a decent midfielder who could play a bit, but was inconsistent and was never going to boss a game of football in a way that Michael Brown or Stuart McCall had, and Andy Taylor a left back from Tranmere. The other paid for signing was Kyle Reid from West Ham who was to go on and make just seven substitute appearances for his reported three hundred and sixty thousand fee before he was moved on to Charlton for free; inspired!

With no more money being released to spend, free transfers Ryan France, Glen Little, Jonathon Fortune and Henri Camara made up the permanent signings while the loan market was used to bring in the likes of Richard Cresswell, James Harper, Keith Treacy, Andrew Davies and Mark Bunn. Bunn was brought in because, as well as selling some of our star players, we lost our star goalkeeper Paddy Kenny early in the season as he was banned for nine months for failing a drugs test which the authorities admitted was because of taking cough medicine, but still gave him what was a season long ban anyway. It could only happen to the Blades.

So the 2009/10 season started with a very different look which was, in my opinion, weaker than the side that were not quite good enough the year before. With the division looking stronger than before, with Newcastle, Middlesbrough and West Brom having come down and Leicester having come up, any thoughts of promotion were merely pipe dreams in the heads of younger Blades fans that had not been around long enough to know any better.

Unbelievably the season started with a six match unbeaten run including a 3-1 win at Reading, who seemed to have stopped being our bogey team, and we were fifth in the table in the company of the four teams mentioned above and a decent Preston side, who had made the play-offs with us the previous season. Of course all good runs come to an end and we lost a tight game 3-2 at Coventry before beating the old enemy at Bramall Lane by the same margin. This was a game where we had raced into a 3-0 lead at half time and everyone was thinking that we were finally going to lay the

Boxing Day ghost to rest but they came back strong at the start of the second half and fought back to make the difference just one goal.

We then managed to go eight games without a win and by just after bonfire night we were down in fourteenth place which to be fair is where I expected us to be given all the changes in the summer. So, just to prove my doubting wrong, the Blades then went on to win four and draw two of their next six games which put them back up to seventh place going into a Boxing Day fixture away at sixth place Leicester. We lost of course.

January fixtures saw us win 1-0 against Middlesbrough and 3-0 over Reading and climb into the play-off zone. The January transfer window also saw us selling Kilgallon and Cotterill and Tottenham reneging on their season long loan agreement and recalling Kyle Walker. Richard Creswell and James Harper's moves were made permanent and Mark Yeats joined from Middlesbrough. Loan deals were also done for Nyron Nosworthy and keeper Steve Simonsen.

Three away defeats and a home draw then had us longing for the away form we had seen the previous year and dropped us into eighth place. Just as last season's away form had helped propel us up the table, this season it was a dreadful run of eight successive away defeats that kept us out of the top six and by the time we picked up out first away point of 2010 at Doncaster, towards the end of March, it looked like there was only the last play-off spot to aim for. We were back in a familiar position of having eight games left and a good run required if our hopes were to be achieved.

A second successive away point at Cardiff kept hopes alive but then a 1-0 home defeat to lowly Scunthorpe followed by a 0-0 home draw with Barnsley effectively, if not mathematically, ended our play-off hopes. After a defeat by leaders Newcastle and a win over Coventry at Bramall Lane we were in tenth place and seven points off the play-offs with just three games left. What we needed was someone to put us out of our misery and to stop the few dreamers that were still around from talking of play-off hopes. That someone came in the shape of our city rivals who held us to a 1-1 draw at Hillsborough and made mathematically certain that we would be in the Championship again the following year. Having being relieved of the pressure of trying to make the top six we then

132

went on to win our final two games, scoring five and conceding nil for an eighth place finish.

There was to be some consolation for us Blades though as the team in blue and white lost their next game at Cardiff City and found themselves relegated to League One. Every cloud etc.

2010/11

The 2010/11 season was to be one where two million pounds was raised in the transfer market by the sale of Billy Sharp to Doncaster and Paddy Kenny to QPR. The Blades had supported Kenny through his ban and cashed in now that he was free to play again. Sharp had proven that he could score at Championship level while on loan at Doncaster and rather than give him a chance to do it for us we again chose a quick buck over longer term success. Also released on free transfers were Little, Camara, Bennett, Harper, Fortune and Naysmith while Derek Geary retired from playing.

With the two million in the kitty we then spent precisely nothing, instead bringing in free signings Daniel Bogdanovich, Leon Britton, Steven Jordan, Johannes Erlt and bringing back Rob Kozluk along with seven loanees. At the time I wondered to myself what the result of such a poor transfer window might be.

The season started with an away draw at Cardiff, not a bad result in the scheme of things. The next game though saw us crash out of the League Cup 2-0 at Hartlepool and when we lost the next League game 3-0 at home to QPR it signalled the end of Kevin Blackwell's time as manager. The official announcement said that he had left by mutual consent which usually means there has been some sort of row between the manager and chairman, but whatever the reasons behind it Blackwell was gone and up stepped Gary Speed into the job that he had been brought in to be groomed for.

Gary had been a good player and a great professional and most people thought that he would make a good manager too. The only doubts in my mind were whether the chance had come too soon. It was pretty clear to me that switching manager's just three games into a season was not a part of the master plan. If it was pre-planned then surely it would have happened prior to the season starting or there would have been some sort of handover plan announced with a future date in mind. As it was the Blades had yet another novice manager and we would have to wait and see how that unfolded.

Speed's reign started with a 1-0 defeat at Middlesbrough but then two 1-0 wins, at home against Preston and away at Derby, gave us a bit of hope and while we were down in twelfth place it was still early in the season and we were only three points off those play-off spots. We were then brought back down to earth with a bang and our weaknesses were exposed for all to see when we were well beaten 4-0 at home to Scunthorpe.

The autumn was a frustrating period as the Blades struggled to put decent back to back results together and it was mid-November before we could boast consecutive wins again with a 1-0 win at Millwall being followed by a 3-2 victory over Palace at the Lane. Two defeats followed and then the Blades were shaken by the news that Gary Speed had been appointed manager of the Welsh national team.

United had been approached by the Welsh FA and, perhaps because of the less than inspiring start to his career at Bramall Lane, had given permission for Speed to talk to them. The Blades had given Speed a three year contract and it was possible that they saw the compensation paid by Wales as a get out of jail card. I am sure that at the time they must have been pondering over whether they had chosen the right man for the job and those thoughts must have swayed them to let Speed go.

We will never know if things would have turned out differently if Speed had remained at Sheffield United, but he did a fine job in starting to turn around the fortunes of his national team before his tragic death, which came less than a year after he left the Blades. I was away on a Caribbean cruise at the time of his death and as the word spread around the fans of a multitude of different teams I could not find anyone who had a bad word to say about the man.

John Carver was appointed acting manager and presided over one win and two defeats before, on the thirtieth of December self-confessed Blades fan Mickey Adams was given the job as manager. Adams started with a defeat at Burnley although after only two days in the job I doubt that he had had time to influence the dressing room for what was our second 4-2 defeat in a row.

Adams first point in for the Blades came in a 2-2 draw at home to Doncaster in a game where, having had a man sent off,

Doncaster then went into a two goal lead with both goals coming from Billy Sharp (who else?) before a late comeback with goals from Bogdanovich and a ninety sixth minute equaliser from Kozluk earning a much needed point. After going out of the cup to Villa another point from a 0-0 draw at Coventry was followed by three successive defeats which left the Blades in the relegation zone.

During the January transfer window Adams had been allowed to spend a little money on centre back Neil Collins and he had brought in a few free transfers with Michael Doyle being the only one that stands out. There were also yet more loan deals done and with Sam Vokes, Marcus Bent, Andy Reid, Joe Mattock and Bjorn Helge Riise all coming from Premier league clubs it looked on the face of it that Adams was adding some quality to the squad. Unfortunately, as we were to find out to our cost, loan players do not always show the full blooded commitment required to be successful in a relegation battle.

Adams start as manager reminded me of the Blades first season in the top flight under Dave Bassett, where we took seventeen games to register our first win. This time it came slightly earlier, but it was still Adams' thirteenth game in charge before he could claim his first win as the Blades manager and in a remarkable coincidence the win came at home to Nottingham Forest once again. A 3-0 defeat at Watford followed but then we won our second home game in a row, beating Leeds 2-0. We were still in the relegation places but these two home victories gave the fans hope that it was starting to come together at last and that survival might still be on the cards.

That hope did not last long and four consecutive defeats left us rock bottom with four games to go and a miracle required. The Blades could have just put us out of our misery, but instead they tore at our emotions by winning the first two of those four games, both by 3-2 margins. This left us with two games to play and a very slight mathematical chance of survival, albeit needing to win two games, see either Doncaster or Crystal Palace lose their two games and see a massive swing in goal difference. Not many people held on to the hope that all three of those things could happen but while ever there was a chance some still dared to believe.

However in our final home game of the season a draw with our near neighbours Barnsley condemned us to a fate that we had probably known was coming several weeks before and we were now heading back to League One. A last day humiliation 4-0 at Swansea was of little relevance and at the end of a season that had seen a boardroom filled with headless chickens, four different managers and the use of forty different players, many of whom did not give a shit about Sheffield United, we had taken a massive step back just twenty four short months after coming so close to a return to the top.

A Big Fish in a Small Pond
2011/12

So we were back in League One and in most people's eyes we were the big fish in this small pond and we were favourites to go straight back up. Having failed to keep us in the Championship Mickey Adams was relieved of his duties and in a somewhat brave move the board had appointed ex Hillsborough player and manager Danny Wilson. I have to say that Wilson himself must have had a pair because he was going to have to do particularly well to win over the majority of Blades fans.

Wilson had famously taken Barnsley to the Premier League for a season, but had less success at Hillsborough managing to help get them relegated, so I suppose we could thank him for that. He had also managed Bristol City where he failed to achieve promotion during his four year stay and he had got MK Dons relegated. He had however managed to get Hartlepool promoted from League Two and Swindon Town to two League One play-off finals so maybe he might just be the right man to manage us at this level of the game.

Having been relegated to League One the transfer business was always going to see the board looking to get money in rather than spend it, so it was no surprise to see an offer of just over a million pounds for young, unproven Jordan Slew accepted and the sale of Jamie Ward and Mark Yeates also brought in close to another million. Several other players were released including Darius Henderson and of course most of the unsuccessful loan players returned from whence they came, personally unaffected by our relegation.

Just one hundred and fifty thousand of the two million quid was reinvested in Ryan Flynn from Falkirk with the rest of the summer business being the free transfer signings of Kevin McDonald (bargain), Chris Porter and Jean-Francois Lescinel. Despite last season's loan disasters our financial situation dictated that more players were brought in on loan to help the cause with Marcus Williams, Nathaniel Mendez Laing, Billy Clarke and Matt Phillips all getting a few games. With Phillips scoring five goals in his five starts for us he was soon sought after and was never likely to become a permanent signing with our restricted budget.

Despite having been relegated the previous season the mood around Bramall Lane was quite positive at the start of the new season with most fans believing we could bounce straight back. The emergence of young Matthew Lowton had been one of few positive points to come out of the previous term and with a young Harry Maguire now in the first team squad and most of the newcomers being in their early twenties the group now had a younger more energetic look.

The season started well with five wins and two draws seeing us stood at the top of the league after the first seven games and the fans starting to warm to the more attractive style of football that the Blades were playing under Wilson. Of course with every wave of optimism United always seem to put the brakes on and three defeats in the next four games saw the heads come out of the clouds and the feet firmly planted back on the ground.

There then followed a 2-2 draw at home in the city derby and a good away result, winning 4-2 at Preston. The unbeaten run was extended to five games, although with the opposition coming in the form of Orient, MK Dons and Exeter we were not getting too carried away, and when we lost the next game at Stevenage (No offence, but, who?) we were given a sharp reminder of exactly where we were in the scheme of things. That result left us in fifth place and, more worryingly, four points behind our city rivals. Maybe our fish was not as big as we thought it was.

The response however was excellent with six straight wins lifting us to second place by the end of the year although a 3-2 defeat at Carlisle in the first game of the New Year saw us swap places with the old enemy in what was becoming an exciting inter-city competition within the bigger picture of our League One campaign.

The winter transfer window saw no money changing hands with just a few loan deals either way but eyebrows were raised when James Beattie, who was now out of contract and without a club, re-joined the Blades.

Two good wins 4-0 at home to Yeovil (again, who?) and 3-0 at Bury saw us back into second spot and then defeat at leaders Charlton saw us drop out of the automatic promotion spot. It was a very exciting time despite being in the third tier and a great contrast to the depressing relegation battle of the previous year.

That loss at Charlton was followed by three wins on the bounce which saw us back in second place and five points clear of the blue and white team, with two games in hand, as we went into the second steel city derby of the season at Hillsborough. Ched Evans had proved to be a revelation at this level, scoring for fun after looking quite ordinary in his two seasons in the Championship. He did however have a cloud hanging over him in the shape of a court case that was coming up around the end of the season but this did not seem to be affecting him and if anything he was playing with the confidence of someone without a care in the world.

That confidence did not help at Hillsborough however and we lost the game 1-0. At the time we did not know just how significant that result would turn out to be, but, come the end of the season, it might be looked at as one of the most significant derby defeats in my time as a Blade. As it was we were still in second place with two games in hand and fifteen games to go.

Although we won the following game we were a little shaken by the derby result and lost the next two games, both 3-2 and the lead over our rivals started to narrow. Wilson however rallied the troops and we went on a run of nine games without defeat, including two 5-2 away wins at Notts County and Rochdale to put us four points clear of our city rivals with just three games to go. Two wins would see us promoted at the first time of asking.

The last game of that unbeaten run was a 3-1 win over Orient at Bramall Lane with the third goal coming from Ched Evans, his twenty ninth league goal of the season, and it may just have been in my mind but his celebration seemed just a little different than his others that season, maybe he knew what was coming. Before the next game, away to MK Dons Ched was due in court to face the charge that had been hanging over him, but not affecting his performances, and everyone was expecting the charges to be proven unfounded and Ched to be back in the team the following day. History however will tell us that was not to be the case and Ched was sentenced to five years in prison.

I had been struggling to get tickets for away games all season due to demand and the loyalty points scheme that led to the same few supporters getting first access to away tickets. I get the idea behind the scheme but I just don't see how anyone is supposed to catch up with those at the top of the list, many of whom buy away tickets to get the points but sell them on rather than actually going to the games. I did however manage to get tickets for MK Dons through just such a route and turned up in Milton Keynes hoping for the win that would put us within touching distance of promotion. In the days before the game I had even had fans of the blue and white shower shaking my hand and conceding defeat in the promotion race.

On the day it was pretty clear as soon as the game kicked off that the player's minds were still in shock from the news of Ched's incarceration the day before and the team stumbled around, pretty much going through the motions rather than going at a Dons team that were there for the taking if only we had tried to take them. We lost the game 1-0 and it was not until the last few minutes that the team really attempted to play the sort of football that had got them where they were in the league. We were still however a point clear of our rivals with a home game against Stevenage up next. A win would still see us in the driving seat on the last day of the season.

Did we get that win? No we did not. It seemed like the loss of Evans had sucked the life out of the team and Stevenage took the lead on thirty one minutes, making a nervous Bramall Lane crowd of thirty thousand even more edgy. Just after half time Stevenage increased their lead to 2-0 and it was apparent that our season was falling apart at the seams. Richard Creswell and Ryan Flynn were brought on for Chris Porter and Stephen Quinn and the Blades went at Stevenage trying to rescue their season. Creswell scored on sixty three minutes and ten minutes later Wilson threw the kitchen sink at it bringing on forward James Beattie for defender Taylor. Beattie had made several appearances for the Blades since his return, mainly as a substitute but had not managed to find the net. Now seemed like the time for him to step up to the plate.

Beattie did not manage to get a goal but we did find an unlikely scorer in full back Matthew Lowton who levelled the game on eighty three minutes. A draw was not going to be enough though and we needed to press for a winner. Press as we might that winner just would not come and we found ourselves going into the last game, away at Exeter a point behind our city rivals knowing that even a win might not be good enough as they were at home to Wycombe Wanderers and were clear favourites for the win that would see them escape League One at our expense.

We drew the game at Exeter and as it turned out a win would not have helped anyway as yet again we ended a season in League One with our biggest enemies taking the promotion spot that should have been ours, but for a poor defence team failing to present the evidence that would have kept Ched Evans out of prison and the Blades in the promotion places. Only Sheffield United could manage to blow their chances in such dramatic fashion time and time again and we were now facing our old nemesis of the play-offs once more.

Fate would have it that we were pitched against Stevenage in the semi-finals (yes I now know who they are!) and a tight but dull away leg saw us return to Bramall Lane for the second leg with the score poised at 0-0. The Blades were still not operating like they had for most of the season and with a disappointing crowd of just twenty one thousand in the ground it was another tight, tense game. Wilson was struggling for strikers and with Evans doing porridge, Creswell nursing a shoulder injury and Beattie suspended he went with the much maligned Chris Porter as a lone striker and five in midfield. Porter was a bit of an anti-hero at the lane and had gone seventeen games without a goal. He had got a few goals in the earlier part of the season but although he was always a willing runner he had been struggling a bit and the crowd had taken to singing *'If Porter scores, we're on the pitch'* in a bit of a micky take of his predicament each time he got a spell in the team.

For eighty four minutes it looked as though it was going to be another game without a goal but then a cross from the right of the pitch was met perfectly by Porter and we were five minutes from a Wembley play-off final. Porter had scored but the fans were not true to their word and stayed off the Bramall Lane turf. Stevenage then threw everything at us, but we managed to hang on and at the final whistle the fans could hold back no more and the kop emptied onto the grass.

We were to play Huddersfield Town at Wembley in what was our sixth attempt at the play-offs and our fourth final. Huddersfield had finished nine points behind us in the league and, on paper; we were the favourites to win the final. After my last visit to a Wembley play-off final I had sworn that I would not attend another one. The combination of our three other play-off finals and three unsuccessful FA Cup semi-final appearances had led me, like many other football fans over the years, to start to wonder if it was my presence at the games that had brought the bad luck. I was also sick of the long drive home filled with disappointment and so I took the decision that not only was I not going to go to the final, but I was also not going to watch the game on TV either. So on the morning of the twenty sixth of May I left my phone in the house, jumped on my motor bike and, with our lass on the back, rode up to Whitby which was pretty much as far away from Wembley as I could get myself.

All day we stayed away from anything that could have informed us of the score and after having a fish and chip dinner we jumped on the bike and headed home, oblivious to the goings on in London. On arrival back home, around seven in the evening, I glanced at the home screen on my phone and, as there were no messages showing from our Steve, I knew that we had lost the game. What I did not know were either the score or the circumstances of the game.

The following day Steve spoke to me and I found out that the game had ended 0-0 and we had lost on penalties. I have still, to this day, never seen any footage of the game or the penalty shoot-out and have no desire to do so. I have been told that the game was as boring as the score line suggests and that the penalty shoot-out was the most drawn out in the history of the play-offs but watching it is not going to change the outcome so what's the point.

I am convinced that if Evans had not been jailed we would have gone up in the automatic places. I am not saying we were a one man team, but the shock of the whole affair knocked the stuffing out of the whole squad and the difference in the style and spirit of our play in the games before and after the event was clear for everyone to see. Things were not made any better when a re-trial some years later found Evans not guilty and although the player will probably see a decent compensation pay out there will be no redress to what that court inflicted on Sheffield United when they made their original decision.

2012/13

So we were still in League One and now without our star striker. Ched had had a remarkable season considering his scoring record prior to the season that had just gone. He had scored just four and nine goals in the two previous seasons and whether it was the lower level he was playing at or he was just a one season wonder no one will ever know. Whatever it was he was gone for the foreseeable future and we needed to regroup and reshape if we were to launch an attack on the top in the 2012/13 season.

Of course there was very little money to spend so it was free transfers that were again turned to, the main one being Dave Kitson, The ginger haired, dirty bastard, formerly with our old bogey team Reading, but now coming to Bramall Lane from Portsmouth. Kitson had been an effective striker (if he was on your team) but at thirty three was getting on a bit so was a bit of a risk. Also coming in on free transfers were Matt Hill who had been on loan the previous year and Tony McMahon a right back from Middlesbrough. Other newcomers were Daryl Westlake, Shaun Miller and Nick Blackman for 'undisclosed' fees.

To make room for the newcomers there was a bit of a clear out with Chris Morgan retiring to take on a full time coaching role under Wilson, star youngster Matthew Lowton was sold to Aston Villa for over three million, Nick Montgomery left for Australia and after just three games of the season Stephen Quinn also left for the mysterious 'undisclosed fee.' Quite a few players were also given free transfers including first team regulars Steve Simonsen, and Lee Williamson. Fringe players Johannes Ertl and Andy Taylor also left on frees and James Beattie, who had been ineffective since his return was released. So it was a different looking squad from the shell shocked ensemble that staggered through the end of the last season.

This particular season started with a sixteen match unbeaten run which put us at the top of the table. Unfortunately half of those games were drawn so while we were top we were not running away with it and only five points separated the top six clubs.

Our first defeat of the season came at MK Dons where it had all started to fall apart the previous season and by an uncanny coincidence the following game was at home to Stevenage, but this time there was no capitulation and we beat them 4-1. Decent results followed and after a 3-0 victory at home to Scunthorpe on Boxing Day we were two points clear at the top.

We were not to kick on however, we are Sheffield United after all, and three home defeats and two away draws followed, plunging us down into sixth place. Time after time year after year the Blades seem to get into the habit of sniffing glory and baulking at the prospect and this was another case of the same.

The January transfer window had seen the arrival of Danny Higginbothom, Barry Robson and Jamie Murphy which on paper looked to have bolstered the squad and going into the spring Wilson looked like he had managed to turn things around. Five wins and two draws in the next seven games saw us climb back up to the second automatic promotion place, but again the dizzy heights must have given the team a collective nose bleed and they got their biggest thrashing of the season in the next game losing 4-0 at Stevenage. Five points from the next three games were not enough to prevent us slipping into fifth place and when we lost the next game at home to Crawley Town (who are these teams?) the board must have thought the writing was on the wall and Danny Wilson was dismissed with just five games of the season left.

Chris Morgan was put in charge until the end of the season, but I was not sure if an untried manager was the answer. The disrupting effect on the team was an unknown factor and given his record over his (almost) two seasons at the Lane, with the best win ratio of any full time Blades manager at that time, I would have thought that Wilson could have seen the job through for the remainder of the season just as well as the novice, even given Morgan's reputation in a battle.

Morgan's first match in charge saw us beat Swindon 2-0 at home, a result that virtually guaranteed a play-off spot and in the next game a 2-2 home draw with Brentford, who were just above us, saw the play-offs become a mathematical certainty, but the two points dropped pretty much ended any hopes of automatic promotion. While we had a game in hand over the top two, making up a six point difference over just three games was never going to happen, not at Bramall Lane anyway.

The relief of making the play-offs must have got to the squad and the last three games produced just one more point in a last day 0-0 stalemate with Preston. Not the ideal build up for the play-offs but we were there in the semi-finals facing Yeovil Town (don't know how many more times I can say 'Who?') in the first leg at Bramall Lane.

The game was unremarkable and a goal from McFadzean just after half time gave us a slender 1-0 lead going into the second leg in a field somewhere in Somerset! This was our seventh attempt at the play-offs and with six previous failures expectations were not high. One thing you can say about the Blades is that they will always try to meet the fans expectations and on a dark day in May they did so once again when they conceded a sixth minute goal to level the tie and then hung on until the eighty fifth minute when a second goal for the minnows from the West Country put us out of our misery and saved us the indignity and expense of yet another Wembley failure.

Yeovil went on to win the final and make it to the Championship for the first and only time in their history. What is the world coming to?

2013/14

For the following season the board had another rush of blood to the head and appointed ex Everton and Rangers defender David Weir as manager on a three year deal. He had previously spent just over a year coaching Everton's academy and reserve teams and the fact that they had not promoted him to manager when David Moyes left ought to have told the board something about his potential. Yet again the future of the Blades was handed to a man with no managerial experience.

Weir had come into the Lane talking of new football philosophies and whatever they were I just wish he could have explained them to the players who seemed to be confused by his approach and tactics throughout his time in charge.

Those players had been shuffled a little since the end of the last season with free transfers being given to Higginbotham, Robson, Creswell and Kitson as well as a couple of fringe players and Kevin McDonald was sold to Wolves after playing just one game.

Coming in were Jose Baxter, Lyle Taylor, Stephen McGinn, Fabian Brandy, and a couple of others whose names made little impression on the team sheet. One or two loan deals were done with Connor Coady being the most notable.

David Weir turned out to be, statistically, United's worst ever permanent manager with just one win and two draws in his time in charge. A win percentage of just 7.69% makes even Martin Peters awful record look good. The only surprise when he was sacked in early October was why it had taken so long. Surprisingly despite our awful start we were still one place above the relegation places, but after the previous two seasons it was the top we were expecting and the Scotsman had probably already seen to it that we would not have to suffer the play-offs again this time.

Morgan was again turned to to look after the team on a temporary basis while a new manager could be found and in his three games in charge he managed a win and a draw which was not exactly promotion form but was a better ratio than Weir had managed.

On the 23rd of October the Blades appointed Nigel Clough as their third manager of the season. With Brian as his dad and a remarkable record as a manager at Burton Albion, where he had taken them from the seventh tier of football to the brink of League two, as well as four years' experience at Derby County he looked like a much better candidate for the job.

Clough arrived with the Blades in the relegation zone and while his start was what can best be described as steady he had managed to get the team to understand what they were supposed to be doing and the ship started to slowly turn around.

The January transfer window gave Clough the opportunity to put his own stamp on the squad but with our league position still being low the money was tight and only the signing of Stefan Scougal troubled the bank manager. Bob Harris was brought in on a free and loan deals found Clough's former Derby players Ben Davies and Kieron Freeman arrive at the Lane. Another loan deal saw Clough bring in his own man for the dressing room in the shape of John Brayford who had been with him at Burton and Derby and 'The Beard' as he became known proved to be a galvanising force at the club.

The Blades had made progress in the FA Cup under Clough, beating Colchester and Cambridge away from home in the first two rounds and he really brought the Blades to the nation's attention when in January we were drawn away yet again this time to top flight Aston Villa and we beat them 2-1 in a pulsating match where our performance belied our third tier status.

We had taken the lead through Jamie Murphy, but when Villa equalised on seventy four minutes most people only expected one result. Ryan Flynn had other ideas though and he belted in a great strike to send the midlands club packing. The cup victory seemed to be a distraction and we lost the next match 2-1 at Notts County and then Drew 1-1 at home to Bradford before the fourth round tie with Premier League Fulham at Bramall Lane. Again we looked well playing against top level opposition and after taking the lead through a Chris Porter goal we were a little disappointed to be pegged back for a 1-1 draw. Before the replay we had the little matter of Crew away and the cup form did not go across to the league with a 3-0 defeat bringing us back down to earth. The replay at Craven Cottage was tight but again we did not look out of our depth against the struggling Premier League side and took them into extra time. As the prospect of penalties loomed we had one more chance as a corner was headed back across the box by Harry Maguire and substitute Shaun Miller stooped to head in for a one hundred and twentieth minute winner which sent us through to the fifth round.

The cup run was fine, but at this point we were still well and truly in the relegation zone. This result however was the one that was the catalyst for a revival in the league and we won the next game against Shrewsbury 2-0 before dispatching Nottingham Forest in the fifth round 3-1 to reach the quarter-finals for the first time in ten years. Suddenly we were playing with a swagger and confidence and we strung together six wins on the bounce to propel ourselves up to twelfth spot and our relegation fears were behind us. We had also beaten Charlton 2-0 in the cup quarter-final and had been drawn to play Hull City, managed by former Blade Steve Bruce at Wembley in the semi.

A mixed bag of results saw us holding our own in mid-table and as we went into the semi-final we were in eleventh place. The semi was played on a Sunday and the kick off was at 4.07 pm, the seven minutes being a mark of respect for the twenty fifth anniversary of the Hillsborough disaster. The late afternoon kick off gave us time to have a day out in London before the game and along with my missus I took son Steve and granddaughter Hannah who had started going to the odd game. After seeing the sights we made our way to Wembley and outside the ground I had my photo taken with Hannah and Mark Labbett, 'The Beast' from TV quiz show The Chase. The Beast is a Blades fan and up close is even bigger than he looks on the TV.

We were a third tier club up against a tidy Hull side who were in the Premier League, but having already dispatched Villa and Fulham we actually fancied our chances that day. We fancied our chances even more after the skilful but unpredictable Jose Baxter gave us the lead on nineteen minutes. We were good value for our lead and were therefore a little disappointed when Hull equalised just before the break. We were back up though just two minutes later when the energetic Stefan Scougal restored our lead and sent us into half time 2-1 ahead.

The second half started and it was clear that Steve Bruce had ripped into his team and they looked much more like the Premiership side that they were and in a disastrous few minutes for the Blades they turned the game around with goals from Fryatt and Huddlestone just five minutes apart putting them into a 3-2 lead. We tried our best to get back into the game but it looked all over on sixty seven minutes when ex-Blade Steven Quinn got a fourth.

As Hull used their top flight experience to manage the ball it seemed to be all over and many Blades fans headed for the tube but then on ninety minutes Jamie Murphy got a third for us and the fans that were leaving flocked back to see if we could force an injury time equalizer. It was not to be though and as we committed bodies forward we left big gaps at the back which Hull pounced upon to wrap the game up with a goal that meant one of the best semi-finals for years had ended up in a 5-3 victory for the Humberside club.

Surprisingly the journey home was not an unhappy one. Although we had lost, we had at last turned up and gave it a go on the big occasion and losing to a side that clearly had the better quality players was no disgrace. Also, Arsenal had made the final a day earlier and while we had given it a good go against some decent Premier League teams it could have been embarrassing had we made it all the way to the final against a top, top team.

It was now just a case of finishing off with a flurry in League One and three wins and two draws from the final five games of the season left us with a seventh place finish which looked out of reach at Christmas and the fans all wondering just what might have been if Clough had arrived earlier. Well next season we may find out!

2011/15

So we were facing our fourth season in League One. When we had been relegated back in 2011 we had expected an immediate return and while we had come close in our first two seasons, reaching the play-offs, we had not managed to make that final step and return to the Championship. The form at the end of the previous season under Nigel Clough had however given us reason to believe that this time we had a chance of going up.

Clough used the summer transfer window to get the squad into the shape he wanted it. Of course the board were looking for some income so our biggest asset of the time, young defender Harry Maguire was sold to the first club that came in with a decent offer and departed for our FA Cup semi-final opponents Hull City. The reported fee of two point eight million seemed to be a snip for such a young, accomplished defender, but we always have been, and probably always will be a 'selling club' and the temptation to refuse mediocre offers for our best players is unlikely to go away anytime soon. Shaun Miller and Matt Hill along with one or two other fringe players were given free transfers and a few others were loaned out to make way for an influx of Clough signings.

Because of our predicament there was obviously very little money to fund this influx so, once again, free transfers were the order of the day, with the most useful ones probably being Chris Basham, Jay McEverly and Craig Alcock. Jamal Campbell-Rice came in and added a little spark now and again. Harrison McGahey a young centre half from Blackpool and Michael Higdon an old fashioned lump of a centre forward from Dutch side NEC Nijmegen came in, with Higdon's signing being accompanied by a rush of views on YouTube of his supposed scoring exploits. The next few months proved to be a testament to the skills of editor of that footage as Higdon struggled to look anything like the player the video had shown. One incoming player did necessitate a trip to the bank as Marc McNulty required just over one hundred thousand pounds to prize him away from Scottish side Livingstone.

So the 2014/15 season started with a different looking squad and an air of optimism around Sheffield 2. As usual it didn't take long for the belief to be tested as we lost our first two League games at home to Bristol City and away at Coventry. We did however successfully negotiate a League Cup first round tie winning 2-1 at home to Mansfield Town.

Things were quickly looking up as we won four and drew one of our next five games in the league and progressed in the League Cup by knocking Premier League West Ham out on penalties after holding them to a draw at the Boleyn Ground. Once again the nations eyes started to turn to lowly Sheffield United's cup exploits.

Our next league game resulted in a 5-2 thrashing at Swindon Town before we dispatched Orient in the next round of the League Cup. A 3-2 defeat at nearby Chesterfield was the only loss in the next six games which included a 2-0 victory at Bradford City. That game was less memorable for the result as for the most ridiculous refusal of a penalty claim ever seen. Stefan Scougal burst into the penalty area and as he tried to evade Bradford defender McArdle he was literally picked up and thrown aside, Sumo style, by the Bradford man as the referee looked straight at the pair from no more than five yards away. Nobody in the ground, or watching on Sky TV, could believe that the ref saw nothing wrong with the challenge and waved away our appeals for a spot kick.

Our cup exploits continued as we won away at MK Dons in the next round of the League Cup and also put Crewe out of the FA cup after a replay. In the league however home defeats by Barnsley and MK Dons slowed our progress and we were down in seventh position at the start of December. It was all still happening in the cups though and wins over Plymouth in the FA Cup and Premier League Southampton in the League Cup quarter-final kept us in the headlines and saw us drawn against Tottenham in a two legged League Cup semi-final with home advantage in the second leg.

League form around this time was not brilliant, but somehow two draws and a Boxing Day defeat at Port Vale saw us end the year in a fifth place play-off spot. The cups had been a distraction, but we seemed to be getting away with it so far and we just needed to do like we had done towards the end of the previous season and turn our cup form into league success.

A busy winter window saw the Blades spend a bit of money with the permanent signing of John Brayford from Cardiff. Brayford had been influential while on loan the previous season and we were hoping that he could do the same again this time round. At just over two million he needed to. Another player who had been on loan the season before, Kieron Freeman was signed up on a free from Derby along with Paul Coutts for the mysterious 'undisclosed sum.' Clough took a bit of a gamble in signing non-league pair Kieron Wallace and Che Adams from Ilkeston Town and also brought in the very lively Matt Done who had been banging in goals at Rochdale. Loan deals for Chris O'Grady, Steve Davis and Jason Holt were also done during the second half of the season.

Before the 2015 league games got under way there was another cup game to attend to and we again made the world sit up and watch as we easily dispatched another Premier League side putting out QPR 3-0 at Loftus Road. I started to think that the style of play that Clough had brought to the Blades was more suited to the higher divisions as we had looked quite comfortable against higher level opposition while we often found it hard going against the more frantic and robust League One teams. This again seemed to be the case as we managed to beat Preston 2-1 but lost 1-0 away to second placed MK Dons leaving us in seventh place in the table as we headed into our League Cup semi-final first leg at White Hart Lane.

This was a different class of Premier League side than we had faced during our previous cup exploits under Clough but we gave it a good shot and the game ended with Spurs holding a slender 1-0 lead to take into the second leg at Bramall Lane and we were still hopeful of turning the tie around in the home leg.

Before that though we had a fourth round FA Cup tie at Preston which we drew 1-1 to force a replay at the Lane. The fixtures were coming thick and fast now and the second leg match against

Tottenham was our fourth game in eleven days and was testing the resolve of the squad. The resolve was there however as the nation watched our attempt to overthrow Spurs and a great game saw a full house witness the emergence of Che Adams as a force to be reckoned with. After conceding an Erickson goal around half an hour into the game we came back to take a 2-1 lead through two goals in two minutes from the novice striker. Extra time was looming and one more goal would see us through to the final but our hearts were broken and our hopes dashed as Erikson grabbed a second goal with just two minutes to go and put Spurs through to the final 3-2 on aggregate. We had however enhanced our reputation in the eyes of the football world once again by going so far in the competition.

Three days later a 2-0 win over Swindon saw us back in the play-off positions and then a 3-1 defeat in the FA Cup replay against Preston meant that we were free to concentrate on the league and our promotion push. A 2-0 defeat at Gillingham was not the best of starts but four wins and two draws in the next six games saw us climb up to third position and with games in hand over those above us we were back into contention for automatic promotion.

We were facing two successive home games against Peterborough and Fleetwood Town and two wins would have surely seen us go to the top. If you have made it this far you will not be surprised to find that we lost both games 2-1 and instead of being in the top two we had dropped to fourth and then two 1-1 away draws saw us in fifth position with Bristol City starting to make a break for it at the top of the table. We did have games in hand but the fixtures were starting to pile up and it was going to be a real test as the season went into its final phase.

Two home wins 1-0 over Port Vale and a resounding 4-0 win against Scunthorpe, who were only two places behind us at the time, raised hopes but then an unexpected 2-1 defeat at home to Crewe dashed those hopes again. Wins over local rivals Barnsley 2-0 away and Doncaster 3-2 at home left us going into the last five games in fifth place, six points behind the automatic spots.

What we needed was to take out now famous cup form into the league and win those five games to give us a chance of avoiding the play-off lottery. A 2-2 draw at Oldham ended any hopes of automatic promotion and then a 1-0 defeat at Yeovil had us starting to worry about our chances of making the play-offs. Our performances had started to become cautions and it seemed that Clough was looking for 1-0 wins and several games towards the end of the season saw the Blades trying to hold the ball by the corner flag rather than attacking the goal. The fans were restless and Clough was starting to be called 'Negative Nigel' as his team seemed to be trying to consolidate and hang on to their play-off spot rather than to kick on and go into the end of season competition on a high. Our cup exploits had seen us playing with freedom and a lack of fear, but now, where that approach should have paid dividends, we were hesitant and scared against teams that ought not to have been able to live with us at our free flowing best and most games were seeing the opposition growing into games as we backed off and hung on.

The final three games were testament to Negative Nigel's approach as we drew all three 1-1 in games where a more bold approach would surely have seen us take maximum points and raise confidence levels. The end of the 2014/15 campaign saw us end in fifth place, twenty one points off the automatic places and no one will ever know if the cup runs helped or hindered our efforts in the league, but I would have gladly exchanged those cup wins for the wins in the league that would have seen us promoted without the need for the dreaded play-offs.

Those play-off games started with a semi-final first leg game against Swindon Town at Bramall Lane and, after a penalty appeal for what looked like a blatant handball by a Swindon defender was turned down, we took the lead through Kieron Freeman. The referee then gave Swindon a penalty after a Swindon player made the most of a Blades defenders dangled leg, but Howard saved the spot kick. We were pegged back just after half time and despite pressing, with Murphy pulling the strings, and a Matt Done goal being ruled out by the referee we could not add to the score to take a lead into the away leg. As most fans were getting their heads around going into the away leg on level terms Swindon had other thoughts and as the clock ticked away their full back carried the ball unchallenged towards our penalty area and a hopeful shot from Twenty five yards went through a crowd of players and nestled in the far corner of the net to give Swindon an injury time winner which meant the game ended in a 2-1 defeat and we had a mountain to climb yet again.

The second leg probably goes down as one of the greatest play-off games of all time, yet it could have been so much more. The poor end of season form seemed to have stuck with us and I watched on in disbelief as in an end to end start we missed our chances while some poor defending saw chances presented to Swindon who gratefully took them and we went 3-0 down after just eighteen minutes. Our eighth play-off competition seemed to have already gone the way of the other seven, but a minute later an own goal gave us the slightest glimmer of hope as the score went to 3-1 on the night and 5-2 on aggregate.

Suddenly it was like we were playing in the cup again and, with nothing to lose, the freedom and flow came back into our play. On thirty eight minutes a diving header from Basham made it 3-2 which remained the score at half time. We were now looking at winning the second half two nil to give us a chance of going through. Not an impossible task, but on fifty nine minutes we were dealt another blow when the ref gave Swindon a penalty after a clumsy attempt to get the ball by keeper Howard and when Swindon scored from the spot kick it looked like our slim chances had gone. Six minutes later though we were back in it as Steve Davis made it 4-3 on the night. We were now going for it, but more poor defending allowed Obika in to score and we thought that was it.

The players had other ideas though and, after the Swindon keeper saved a long range shot, Matt Done pounced on the loose ball to make it 5-4. Then with the time ticking away Che Adams powered through the defence and slammed home an equaliser.

We desperately needed one more goal to take it to extra time. With nearly three minutes of extra time gone Adams ran at the defence again and after brushing aside a despairing defender fired the ball into the goal for what we thought was our sixth goal. The referee though soon put an end to our celebrations as he blew his whistle and awarded Swindon a free kick, deeming that Adams had fouled the defender on the edge of the box as he had tried to block Adams run. To be fair it was one of those that you have seen given and seen let go depending on how different referees might have viewed it. I was furious with the ref at the time, but having seen replays of the incident I would probably have wanted the foul given if it had been a Swindon player going through our defence in the same way. The game ended shortly afterwards and a thrilling 5-5 draw saw neutrals raving about the game and Swindon go through, courtesy of their injury time winner in the first leg, and a good season ended yet again in play-off misery.

2015/16

It took the board just two weeks to decide that Clough had failed to do the job he had been asked to do, namely get us promoted, and his services were disposed of. His record had been pretty good and he had raised the profile of the club with those cup runs, but at the end of the day we were still in the third tier of English football and that was not good enough.

A new manager was required and as a long list of potential candidates circulated on the rumour mill it took the board just a week to announce the news that Nigel Adkins was our new manager. Adkins had gained three promotions from League one, taking Scunthorpe United up twice and getting Southampton promoted to the Championship then taking the Saints straight up into the Premier League. He had more recently been less successful overseeing Reading's relegation from the Premier League and watching them struggle back in the Championship. Fans were not sure if his bubble had burst, but he talked a good game so time would tell.

We had failed to get promoted so the tradition of selling our best player continued when Jamie Murphy was transferred to Brighton after just one game for what seemed to be a very cheap one point nine million pounds for such a gifted player. Ageing pair Ben Davis and Michael Doyle were given free transfers. As there appeared to be no one interested in taking the hapless Higdon away from us on a permanent basis he was loaned to Oldham Athletic and a bunch of younger prospects were loaned out to gain experience.

Surprisingly some money was given to Adkins which he used to bring Billy Sharp back to Bramall Lane for his third spell with the team he loved. Sharp had played for Adkins at Scunthorpe, Southampton and on loan at Reading and, as well as being a season ticket seller, the move also put an Adkins man at the heart of the dressing room. Also coming in were Martyn Woolford from

155

Millwall while the loan signings of Dean Hammond, Connor Salmon and David Edgar gave the team a different look.

The 2015/16 season could not have got off to a worse start with a 4-0 defeat coming at Gillingham on the opening day. The Blades rallied though and a narrow League Cup victory at Morecombe was followed by three league wins in a row. We then went out of the League Cup 3-0 at Fulham, where we had had cup success under Clough, and then a fourth successive league win, 2-0 at Swindon saw us in second position with twelve points from five games. It's a pity we could not have got that 2-0 win just a few months earlier, we might have been playing in the Championship now instead of losing our next two home games 3-2 to Colchester and 3-1 to Bury.

Our form was not good and by the end of October we were down in eighth place in the table with just seven wins from our sixteen games. Not exactly promotion form. Three draws and a 4-2 home defeat by Shrewsbury in November did not help and we went into December in twelfth place. December was a better month with three wins out of three but our Boxing Day game at Wigan was postponed when we were in good form and, who knows, if it had been played when scheduled it could have been four from four.

After a 3-2 loss at home to Peterborough the rest of January saw us go four games unbeaten, although three of those games ended in draws and as it turned out our seventh place at the end of the month was going to be the highest we achieved for the remainder of the season. However we almost had another highlight in the FA Cup when we held Man United for ninety three minutes at Old Trafford before a Wayne Rooney penalty put an end to any hopes of further cup glory.

January also brought another transfer window and an opportunity to strengthen, but with the writing seemingly already on the wall the only incoming business was the loan of Alex Baptiste and the extension of Dean Hammonds' loan. We did manage to offload Higdon to Tranmere and Neil Collins went to the USA on a free while other players were loaned out, including Marc McNulty which was a bit of a surprise as while Sharp and Adams were getting among the goals there was very little goal threat from anywhere else. I presume his face did not fit.

Two wins and four defeats in the next six games consigned us to twelfth place and we pretty much knew that our season was over. Adkins had proved to be uninspiring and, while he always presented himself well, he seemed to lack any real passion and came across as a bit of a wet lettuce when interviewed on TV. What we really needed was someone who could get into the players and squeeze the best out of them. Adkins was certainly not a Bassett or Warnock and some of the Blades displays were reflecting his 'nice' personality when what was needed was some battle and fight. Give me a manager in a track suit rather than a Saville Row suit any day.

Just two wins in March did nothing to inspire thoughts of a late push for the play-offs and while there was a little flurry in April with three wins and two draws in a five game unbeaten run we lost our last two games to end the season in a disappointing and unacceptable eleventh place and Adkins was gone within days.

One of Our Own
2016/17

Before Adkins had been appointed a name had been bandied about among supporters speculating on who the next boss might be. The name was that of our former right back Chris Wilder. Wilder had been quietly making a name for himself managing Alfreton Town, Halifax Town, Oxford United and Northampton Town with some success on budgets too low to even be called shoestring. At that point though the board must not have been convinced and appointed the more established figure of Adkins.

Wilder had done remarkably well at Northampton in particular where he had joined them as they looked odds on for relegation to the Conference and as Adkins was making the Blades worse, Wilder transformed Northampton into League Two champions despite a financial background that had seen wages going unpaid at times. After managing three 'Towns' it seemed it was now time for him to come back to the big city.

The Blades almost missed out on their man though as his exploits had also been recognised by Charlton Athletic who had also decided that they wanted Wilder as their next manager. I don't know how true it is, but it has been reported that Wilder was actually in the Charlton office when the call came through from Bramall Lane offering him the job, but once offered it turned out to be irresistible for the former fan, ball boy and player and Wilder was appointed as manager of the club he has always loved.

Where other managers often liked to bring in their own favourites to be their man in the dressing room Wilder saw no reason to as he had the perfect candidate there already and one of his first acts was to make fellow lifelong Blade Billy Sharp club captain. One of the main things the Blades had seemed to lack under the leadership of Adkins was passion, but now we had a manager and a captain that understood our club, its fans and its history.

Wilder did of course need to reshape the squad to help him develop his own style of play and in the summer window he had a massive clear out of players to make way for incoming transfers. The Blades had not suddenly come into loads of money so cash was raised yet again by selling two of our brightest prospects in Che Adams and Dominic Clavert-Lewin raising around three and a half million pounds. Adams was starting to look like he would develop into a good striker, but apparently he was unsettled, while with just three league starts and six substitute appearances Calvert-Lewin was another of those 'too good to refuse the offer' sales that we had become used to. Amongst those released on free transfers were the likes of Jamal Campbell-Rice, Ryan Flynn, Mark Howard, Florent Cuvelier, Jay McEverley, Martyn Woolford and Harrison McGahey while McNulty, and Brayford were sent out on loan. Other players were released including Jose Baxter who had got himself into a little trouble outside the game.

Incoming transfers included Simon Moore for just over half a million, Jack O'Connell, Leon Clarke and Caolan Lavery for undisclosed sums along with free signings John Fleck, Jake Wright, and Mark Duffy. Loan deals were also done for Daniel Lafferty, Ethan Ebanks-Landell and a young Harry Chapman. Wilder certainly did not mess about and while most of his signings were relatively unknown among Blades fans we were soon to find out that our new manager had an eye for a certain type of player.

There was a good feeling amongst the fans going into the season and with a whole new look to the squad we went into the 2016/17 season with a level of expectation that belied the previous seasons poor performance. The fans however soon became a little restless as just one point from the first four games saw us rock bottom of the early season table. The team seemed to be struggling to get used to Wilder's new style of play and in the early season games there would regularly be three or four players down one of the channels with just one body in the box to aim at and while possession was high chances were few and far between.

Wilder however knew what he wanted from the team and after changing to three at the back he persevered with the tactics he wanted the Blades to play. I have been told that after the fourth fixture, a 2-1 defeat at Millwall, Wilder took the team out for a night on the piss in order to raise their spirits (in more ways than one). Whether this is true or not, whatever Wilder did had the right effect and as the players started to understand what was being asked of them they set off on a run of fifteen unbeaten games which included eleven wins and with Duffy looking a class above most players in the division and Billy Sharp finding the net regularly we played most games on the front foot. Paul Coutts had taken up a holding role in midfield and looked a much better player for it and fans were amazed as not just our wing backs but our central defenders, Jack O'Connell in particular made regular surges down the flanks.

This was a great time to be a Blade and despite giving the rest of the league four games start we were now clear favourites for that elusive promotion back to the Championship. A 1-0 home defeat to Walsall ended the unbeaten run, but that only seemed to spur the team on and the next six games were all wins as we took eighteen points from eighteen going through December and into January.

Our form suggested that we did not need to do much business in the January transfer window but Wilder tinkered around the edges making Lafferty's loan deal into a permanent move and adding Samir (six touch) Carruthers and bustling striker James Hanson to the squad as well as doing loan deals for Jay O'Shay and Joe Riley while one or two fringe players were released or loaned out.

The six game winning run was ended again by Walsall who thumped us in the return fixture at their ground 4-1. Walsall were the only team that seemed to be able to counter our new style of play and I must take my hat off to their manager Jon Whitney who found the team and the tactics to become the only side to do the double over Wilder's Blades in this remarkable season. The Walsall defeat was followed by a stuttering 2-2 draw against Gillingham at the Lane and then a shock 2-0 home defeat to Fleetwood Town and we ended January with a little niggle in the back of my mind that the wheels may be about to come off, as they had in the second half of a few other seasons.

As if my doubts had somehow echoed around the dressing room of Bramall Lane the team soon put those doubts to rest by setting off on another unbeaten run and by the time we had made that run ten games long it was no longer a case of if we would be promoted but simply a matter of when. Two more games and two more wins later and we were on the verge of not only promotion but also the title and as tickets for the next game, away to Wilders old club Northampton Town were as rare as rocking horse shit the

Blades were granted permission to beam-back live coverage of the game to Bramall Lane. As I was still struggling to get tickets for away games under the well-meant but slightly flawed loyalty points scheme I had to make do with tickets for the beam-back at Bramall Lane and sat in the John Street stand in a slightly unusual atmosphere as fans cheered at the unhearing screens located on the edge of the pitch.

The game itself was a little edgy as the expectation seemed to sit just a little heavily on the player's shoulders. Although Carruthers hit the bar and an effort from Coutts sailed just over the top there was not too much else to report and when Northampton took the lead just before half time it looked as though we might have to wait a little longer for our promotion to be confirmed. The second half was better though and the players grew in confidence and started to knock the ball around with more of the freedom that we had been used to seeing for most of the season and when Leon Clarke found the net on the hour mark we were as good as there.

A win would be better than a draw however and the Blades went for another as the fans packed in behind the goal in Northampton and in front of the screens at Bramall Lane willed them on. Then in the eighty eighth minute a cross from Billy Sharp found John Fleck, who had had an outstanding first season, bursting into the box and Fleck took the ball a couple of yards forward and slotted it under the Northampton keeper to make sure with a second goal for a 2-1 victory. The goal was greeted with a mini pitch invasion, which was nothing to the scenes that were to follow the final whistle when the whole away following took to the Northampton pitch and raised captain Billy Sharp on their shoulders, while at Bramall Lane the empty pitch was also invaded by many of the crowd that had watched the beam-back. After six years in League One we were finally back up into the Championship.

The season was not over though and there were still four games to go. The team could have been forgiven for relaxing a bit and coasting to the end of the season but Wilder was having none of it. The Northampton result had left us on eighty eight points and with twelve points still available there was a chance to set a club record by hitting the magical one hundred point mark and so that was now the target to motivate the players. The players responded in style with 3-0 wins in the first two of those games, away at Port Vale and at home to Bradford. MK Dons were up next and, after our glorious failure at Milton Keynes following the Ched Evans affair, this was the fixture everyone wanted to go to and there was an almighty clamour for tickets. Despite the MK Dons ground having a whole upper tier that remained empty for most games the Dons would not give in to the Blades request for more tickets and in doing so must have lost an awful lot of potential income. I'm sure we could have filled the ground for that game. I would have qualified for a ticket with my main season ticket's loyalty points but could not get two tickets because there were fewer points on my second season ticket. I did not want to leave the missus at home, so while the lucky ones manged to get to the game I had to make do with TV clips and fans video footage to try and pick up on the atmosphere as hordes of Blades invaded Milton Keynes and marked the last away game in League One with joyous singing, conga lines and bright red flares as yet another 3-0 victory lifted us on to ninety seven points.

The last game of the season was against already relegated Chesterfield at Bramall Lane and the magic one hundred points was still on the cards. Thirty one thousand packed into the ground to cheer on the champions, but although the Chesterfield players gave the Blades a guard of honour as they entered the pitch, they were not in any mood to make it easy for us and even had us kicking towards the kop in the first half rather than the second which is the tradition. It did not throw us though and on eighteen minutes Kieron Freeman made it 1-0 with his tenth goal of the season.

Chesterfield were not going to roll over though and almost on the stroke of half time they scored a penalty after Simon Moore had brought down one of their forwards, so it was back to square one for the start of the second half. On fifty nine minutes Billy Sharp rose to meet a cross and headed in his thirtieth league goal of the season and it looked like the one hundred points was on again, but Chesterfield made a mockery of their bottom place in the table and pegged us back yet again when they levelled on sixty five minutes and we had to start all over again. Our cause was helped however as while the Chesterfield fans celebrated their equaliser they had a man sent off for something I must have missed.

Playing against ten men is not always easy though and Chesterfield held on until the eighty second minute when Daniel Lafferty rolled a lazy shot from eighteen yards into the bottom corner to wrap up a 3-2 win and those precious one hundred points. The crowd stayed off of the pitch this time so that the presentation of the League One trophy could be made and the fans sang about Jack O'Connell's magic hat, amongst other things, as flames and confetti flew up in the air. We had given the rest of the division four games start, had won the league with four games left and finished fourteen points clear of the nearest contenders. That is what I call a good season.

The celebrations did not end that day though and later that week an open topped bus ferried the players and management to the town hall for a civic reception to honour the Blades. As throngs of Blades fans lined the street Chris Wilder, beer in hand, nearly fell off the top deck and once on the town hall balcony Kieron Freeman had the crowd looking on anxiously as he walked along the top of the balustrade half drunk. The best bit though, at least for anyone with a sense of humour as wicked as mine, was when most of the team sung along in front of the gathered dignitaries *"Jack O Connell's magic, he wears a magic hat, and if you throw a brick at him he'll head the fucker back etc."* The council officers did not know where to look and I'm sure it will be a long time before they lay on another posh do for one of the local football teams.

2017/18

We were now back in the Championship and although we had walked away with the title the previous season this was a different level to what we had been used to, so most fans were probably expecting us to struggle a little as we tried to consolidate our position in the 2017/18 season.

The Championship is probably the most competitive of all the divisions and any team can beat any other team on their day, so success is about consistency and concentration as well as ability and a little rub of the green. We would also be competing against teams with bigger and better resources than we have at our disposal and there is also the unfair advantage in spending power

164

posed by the clubs that have recently come down from the Premier League with their parachute payments, as well as the clubs with richer and more ambitious owners who can splash around the sort of money that we can only dream of.

The board must also have realised that we had a job on our hands and for the first season for some time we spent much more than we received in the transfer market. It was not hard to do as those players leaving the Blades did so for free. Scougal, McNulty, Done, Kieran Wallace and John Brayford all departed for no income. On the plus side, our better players were signed up on new contracts rather than being sold to the highest bidder and it looked like for once we were building rather than dismantling a squad.

As for incoming players, Wilder surprised me, if no one else, as he brought in two new wing backs in the shape of George Baldock and Enda Stevens. We had bossed League One with Lafferty and Freeman performing well in the wing back positions, but the manager was clearly intent on upping the stakes with competition for places. Also coming in were Nathan Thomas (a bit of a punt on a young winger from Hartlepool, who had just been relegated out of the League) Richard Stearman from Fulham, John Lundstram from Oxford and, in a bit of a turn up, Ched Evans who had by now had his conviction overturned. Ched had done a season at Chesterfield, but no one really knew if his time spent at her majesty's pleasure would have robbed him, and us, of his best years in the game, but there was unfinished business to be done so time would tell. Clayton Donaldson and Ben Henegan were signed towards the end of August and Jamal Blackman and Cameron Carter-Vickers were signed on season long loans from Chelsea and Spurs respectively. In total the board had invested almost four and a half million, which is peanuts compared with most of the teams we would be up against but was a fortune by our standards.

The first game of the season was at home to a Brentford team that had finished in tenth position the previous season and were considered to be a decent side, so it would be a good measure of where we were. A good crowd of over twenty seven thousand generated a fantastic atmosphere as they welcomed the Blades back into the Championship and the team responded by performing well enough to win the game 1-0 with a goal from our captain Billy Sharp. The next game was away to Middlesbrough and, in a televised game, I thought the Blades gave the high spending opposition far too much respect and did not play with their usual positive approach for long enough during the game. 'Boro scored after a poor attempt at an headed clearance. Although the Blades came back into it, and had what looked like a perfectly good goal ruled out by the officials right at the end, I have to say that we were probably just not good enough, for long enough, to come away with anything on the day.

In the next game at Cardiff we were definitely not good enough against a well organised Neil Warnock side and we could have few complaints about the 2-0 defeat. This was a Chris Wilder side though and the response to two away defeats was to win the next four games on the bounce, including a fine 3-1 win at home to Derby County who were, as usual, fancied to be promotion contenders and a 2-1 win at Sunderland where Clayton Donaldson scored two excellent goals. Suddenly we were up to third in the table and starting to believe we belonged there. For the next game I was away on holiday again and I managed to pick up a live stream of the match and witnessed the most blatant and contemptible display of timewasting and negative play I can remember seeing, by a Norwich side that ought to be ashamed of themselves.

Norwich had taken the lead, against the run of play, in the twenty third minute and had been very slow in their play well before then. After the goal they made very little attempt to come at us and as we dominated possession they took game management and sportsmanship way beyond acceptable limits as they took ridiculous amounts of time to restart the game at every throw in, goal kick and free kick, aided and abetted by a referee who took no action against their very obvious time wasting tactics until very late in the game and it ended in a 1-0 defeat and a lot of animosity between the managers.

I am not of the opinion that teams should just come and roll over and I am not naïve enough to think that there will not be times that we will need to shut up shop and manage the back end of games to pick up the points we need, but this was pushing things way beyond game management and was a shameful display by a side that are capable of much better than that and the thought of their display that day leaves a bad taste in the mouth.

There was no time to dwell on our misfortune though as the next game was against our bitter rivals at Hillsborough and after five years without a meaningful derby game both sides were giving it large around town. Back from my holiday, but with away tickets quickly sold out again, I was grateful that the game had been selected for live coverage by Sky TV and I settled down in front of the TV with our lass and our Steve hoping for the best and praying that there would be no humiliating defeat.

It seemed that both my hopes and prayers were answered when, just Three minutes in, exciting young prospect David Brooks was felled on the edge of the box as he skipped through the oppositions defence. As they lined up a wall expecting a direct shot on goal Brooks cleverly rolled the ball backwards to John Fleck who, with a clear sight of goal, slammed the ball home from twenty five yards for an early opener. It got even better on fifteen minutes when, as the blue shirted team tried to attack, Enda Stevens played a long ball over the top and Leon Clarke, returning to one of his old clubs, caught the opposition defence napping and dashed through to slot home a second from the edge of the box.

We were 2-0 up, but city pride was at stake and they pressed for the goal that would get them back into the game and just as we were expecting the half time whistle Gary Hooper scored his one hundredth league goal to give the home side some hope.

The second half started with us under a little bit of pressure, but when in possession Brooks was giving their defence a torrid time and he played a part in the build up to a chance for Leon Clarke to net what he thought was his second goal. The linesman however ruled it out, deeming that Chris Basham had strayed off side before crossing to Leon. It was end to end stuff and Clarke had a chance to wrap it up when Brooks brilliantly bamboozled and nutmegged a sorry looking defender and crossed to the unmarked striker who managed to put his easiest chance of the game over the bar.

We were then put under some pressure with our opponents looking to exploit space in wide positions and they levelled when a cross found Joao in the box and he slammed home an equaliser from twelve yards. The home fans went wild and it seemed that almost everyone in the ground (other than those in red and white obviously) was stood up and bouncing and, if it wasn't for the fact that I hate them with a passion, I might even be persuaded to say it looked good.

With the reversal in fortunes the home fans and the TV commentators must have thought that there was only going to be one winner from here. Mark Duffy however was having none of it and almost immediately from the kick-off he received the ball mid-way in the opposition half and laid it back to Leon Clarke. Clarke played a lovely first time ball over the top of the home defence into the path of Duffy who took the ball into the box and turned the defenders inside out before firing home from the tightest of angles to restore the Blades lead. The previously exuberant home fans were now silent and the noise was coming from the Blades fans high up in the Leppings Lane stand as they sung '*You're not bouncing any more*' to their rivals.

Brooks then turned the defence inside out and produced a fine save from keeper Westwood and on seventy seven minutes Brooks and Clarke combined to see Clarke burst between two defenders and chip the ball over the advancing keeper and wrap the game up at 4-2. When the final whistle went the Blades fans celebrated and taunted their rivals with chants of '*The city is ours*' which it certainly was that day.

The following game was a real test against a classy Wolves side who were almost everyone's favourites for the title having invested a lot of money in quality players and a good manager in Nuno Espirito Santo. We were helped by the fact that former Blade Connor Coady was sent off early in the game and Ruben Neves missed a penalty, but even so we did not look out of place in this sort of company and another two goals from Leon Clarke, who was in the form of his life, wrapped up a 2-0 victory to put us into second place in the table.

A 2-1 defeat at Nottingham Forest in a televised game that no one to this day can explain how we lost, such was our dominance, was followed by three straight wins, the third of which was another live TV game at Leeds where Billy sharp put us ahead in the second minute and a Leeds equaliser made it level until second half substitute David Brooks scored with a delightful finish to give us three precious points at our Yorkshire rivals. A loss at QPR was quickly followed by a 4-1 thumping of Hull City at Bramall Lane with Clarke getting all four goals. Then came what was to me the turning point in our season.

We were playing away to Burton Albion on a freezing cold Friday night and as I had a friend who lived in Burton I had managed to get tickets in the home section of the ground. It was my first visit to Burton and I must say that I was quite impressed with the set up at their very small but well run stadium. Billy Sharp opened the scoring with a penalty after ten minutes and a spirited Albion side managed by former Blades manager Nigel Clough gave a good show and equalised on thirty two minutes. Sharp restored the lead three minutes later, but the blow that was to have serious consequences for the Blades hopes came when Paul Coutts attempted a shot from the edge of the box and his swinging leg followed through to collide with the foot of a Burton defender who was desperately trying to get at the ball. I was sat in the stand, level with where Coutts was, and could hear the crack as Coutts leg snapped. There were a few heated words after the game about the legitimacy of the defenders challenge, but from where I was sat he was making a genuine attempt to get the ball and it looked like an unfortunate coming together. If the defender had not made the challenge then you would have to question why he was on the pitch.

Leon Clarke added a third goal in the second half to give the Blades a 3-1 win and send them top of the league, at least overnight, but the result was overshadowed by the injury to Coutts who was out for the rest of the season. Coutts had been hugely influential in our promotion year, and in the season to date, holding the midfield in front of our back three and providing a platform for our wing backs and centre halves to overlap down the flanks. While no player is irreplaceable, the squad at that time lacked anyone who could play in that role with the same calm authority that Coutts had shown and it took a while for the team to find the sort of shape and form that had been there before the loss of Coutts and probably, ultimately, cost us points that may have seen a different result come the end of the season. Before I move on I must give out a big shout to John Brayford who, although he was by then a Burton player, accompanied his former team mate to the hospital and stayed with him throughout the night. A true mate.

169

We were not a one man team, but the role that Coutts had been playing takes a certain type of player and we were soon to find out that our squad lacked another one. The next game was a home game against a Fulham side that had just missed out on promotion to the Premier League the previous year. They had not started this season very well and were down near the bottom of the table but were still a very good side.

As the match started we were on our game going forward, but, even before we went a goal up through Leon Clarke, Fulham were showing a turn of pace and swiftness in passing that was catching our defence out every time they got the ball. They were happy to let us have possession in our own half and around the half way line but as we approached the final third they would press to gain possession and then in just two or three passes they were closing in on our goal. Two goals in two minutes around the half hour mark, both following mistakes from Carter-Vickers, gave them the lead and, while Clarke equalised on thirty nine minutes, a Fulham goal four minutes later saw us go in 3-2 down at half time.

Without an experienced holding midfield player we were far too open and the second half was just the same with end to end football seeing us stretched each time Fulham came forward and they raced into a 5-2 lead as our defenders were left isolated time and again. We were not done though and, in what must have been a brilliant game for the neutral, as Fulham tried to see out the game we gave it another push and Carruthers made it 5-3 on eighty six minutes. We threw the kitchen sink at them and in the first minute of injury time Clarke completed his hat trick to make it 5-4. If there had been another few minutes of injury time we may have even levelled it but as it turned out Fulham took all the points in one of the most exciting games played at the Lane for years.

John Lundstram had been brought in to replace Coutts, but he is a different sort of player altogether and in my opinion, although I'm sure Wilder will not necessarily agree, while he is a willing runner and would never give less than one hundred percent, he looks like he has found himself in a division higher than where he is comfortable.

We struggled to regain our style and the next four games saw three defeats and a solitary point at home to Birmingham. We were then at Aston Villa in a game shown on Sky TV and it looked like another bad day at the office when Villa raced into a two goal lead within nine minutes. The blades then rallied and two goals from Clayton Donaldson made it 2-2 with less than half an hour played. It looked like it might turn into another Fulham game but the match settled down and no more goals were scored and we were grateful for an away point given the start we had.

A win and a draw then set us up for the second Steel City Derby of the season as we faced the other lot at Bramall Lane. This game was quite open considering that bragging rights were at stake and while we dominated the game for periods we allowed them too much time when they had the ball. Both sides had chances and if I am honest they could have won it but for a fantastic save from Simon Moore in the closing stages. At the end of the day a 0-0 draw was probably (begrudgingly) a fair result.

Either side of that derby game Wilder had dipped into the transfer market bringing in long term targets Ryan Leonard and Ricky Holmes, but the best bit of business was probably the acquisition of midfielder Lee Evans from Wolves (although he had been playing on loan at Wigan). Evans was a better fit in the centre midfield roll and once in the team he started to add a bit of the stability in front of the defence that had been missing since we had lost Coutts.

We had had a pretty average time since hitting the top of the league after the Burton game and we had only won once in the ten games since, but were surprisingly still in sixth position. Our next game however ended that particular poor run and gave an immense amount of pleasure to most Blades fans when we went to Norwich and won 2-1 with the final minutes being accompanied by the Blades fans singing.' *Take your time, take your time Sheff United; take your time, take your time I say: Take your time, take your time Sheff United. Play your football the Norwich way.*' In reference to their time wasting charade earlier in the season.

We could not seem to buy a draw in the next seven games with the first of those games being against Villa at home and seeing us concede a last minute goal after totally dominating the game. While we picked up wins at home against Leeds and QPR we were totally outclassed 3-0 at Wolves and also lost 3-0 at Fulham who had had a remarkable run since beating us and were now promotion contenders. Draws in either of those games would have been very valuable points, but the worst result came at Hull where we just did not show up and lost a game 1-0 to a side that we should have been taking to the cleaners.

From not being able to buy a draw we then went on to draw four of our next five games when we should have taken all three points in three of those games. The final one was a 1-1 draw at home to Cardiff who, despite being among the favourites to go up, were well outplayed and scraped a point with an injury time equaliser. Their manager Neil Warnock was gracious enough to admit that they had gotten away with it on the day, that sort admission being something that is seldom seen from our former manager.

We had by now dropped to ninth position and after losing 3-2 at Barnsley we had just five games left and were facing an uphill task if we wanted to make the play-offs. That task started with a home game against Middlesbrough and two fine goals from Lee Evans helped us to a 2-1 win over the big spending Teesiders, but we could not follow it up in the next game when we let Millwall straight back into the game after taking the lead in a hard fought match.

The long season was catching up on our squad which was shown to be lacking the depth required to make it all the way and two defeats, at home to Birmingham and away to Preston, saw the last of our dwindling play-off hopes gone. A final day 3-2 result at Bristol City saw our first season back in the Championship end with a win and a creditable tenth position finish just six points off the play-offs. Considering our expectations at the start of the season, our limited resources and a bit of bad luck on the way it was a great first season back and with Wilder at the helm we were rearing to go again next time.

2018/19

The lack of depth that had ultimately been our undoing needed to be addressed and, despite a behind the scenes battle for control of the club dragging on, the board tried to operate the business as usual. David Brooks had been a revelation in the games that he had played allthough a bout of glandular fever had meant that he had not had as many games as most Blades would have liked to have seen. It had been enough however to alert a number of Premier League clubs. Wilder had tried to persuade the youngster

172

to stay with the club and develop his game over another season but the attention from the top tier had started to turn his head and it was probably inevitable that he would go. Liverpool and Spurs had both been rumoured to have been interested so it came as a bit of a surprise when it was Eddie Howe's Bournemouth that landed the player. It was also a bit of a surprise when rumours that the 'undisclosed fee' was as little as ten and a half million went round. I am sure time will tell that we have given away yet another good player for well under his true value. I hope there is a good sell on clause.

Clayton Donaldson ended his brief spell at Bramall lane when he was released. And the fringe squad was tidied up with Hanson, Hussey, Reid and Long all leaving for pastures new.

Players deemed surplus to immediate requirements, but with no immediate buyers stepping in, were loaned out and included Samir Carruthers, Ben Henegan, Nathan Thomas, Ched Evans and January signing Ricky Holmes. There was also a bit of a surprise when Lee Evans expressed an interest in moving back to Wigan and a loan deal was done. When Ryan Leonard was loaned to Millwall at the end of August it seemed that Wilders previous January deals had all been flops.

Despite the decent season before and the sale of Brooks there was not much money flying around and the signing of John Egan from Brentford was the only major spending with the fee again 'undisclosed' but thought to be around four or five million. Other signings were less high profile with David McGoldrick coming from Ipswich on a free, with a question mark over his fitness. Young Manchester City prospect Kean Bryan was signed on a free and as the transfer window drew to a close the fans were underwhelmed by the announcement that we had signed Connor Washington on a free from QPR. Martin Cranie was signed at the last minute to provide cover in defence and, with biggest signing Egan still getting used to playing in a back three, no one was getting too carried away with Mr Wilder's shopping spree.

The loan market was a different thing and we were delighted to welcome Dean Henderson from Manchester United and Oliver Norwood from Brighton. Norwood had been promoted to the Premier League in both the previous two seasons and we were hoping that he was going to make it three in a row with us. The

Norwood loan was done with a view to making it a permanent deal in January and looked to be the best of the deals done. The other deal that had fans looking on with interest was the loan signing of young Liverpool starlet Ben Woodburn. He was a Wales teammate of David Brooks and was tipped to become a Liverpool star of the future so he came with great expectations. The last of the summer loan signings was Marvin Johnson from Middlesbrough and I don't think it would be too much of a spoiler if I told you now that Wilder shouldn't have bothered. Young Reece Norrington-Davies had been used in some of the pre-season games and in my opinion he would have been a much better back up to Enda Stevens than the 'Boro reject.

So with the business done the 2018/19 season got underway and again it was a slow start for Wilders men with a home loss to Swansea in a game we should have won and a 3-0 defeat at Middlesbrough in a game that was brought forward at their request and, on reflection, should have been left where it was first scheduled. We then kicked into winning mode with four wins on the trot. The last of which was a brilliant 4-1 victory over Aston Villa at Bramall Lane in a match where we totally outplayed their 'star studded' team and the smug figure of Jack Grealish was taunted with the chant of '*You should have fucked off to Tottenham*' as the game drew to a close, after he had put on a far better display of diving than he did of playing football.

A goalless draw at home to Birmingham was followed by four more wins on the bounce and after twelve games we found ourselves briefly at the top of the table. We then went to Derby County and after conceding a first minute goal we outplayed the home side and went in at half time level at 1-1 after Basham had equalised. This was yet another game shown live on the TV and all the pundits were raving about our play and expecting us to go on and win the game. Inexplicably we came out for the second half and sat back seemingly determined to hang on to the draw rather than go for the win that was there for the taking. Derby couldn't believe their luck and grew into the game and it was no surprise when Marriott knocked in a winner on seventy seven minutes.

There had been a few occasions under Wilder where the Blades had been in a good position, but for some reason had dropped deeper and invited pressure rather than playing their confident,

174

front foot, attacking style and I have no idea if it is a tactic encouraged by the manager or just a mentality that settles on the collective group when we are ahead, but my fingernails are constantly bitten down to the quick when I should be seeing out most games happy in the knowledge that we are going to win.

The next stage of the season was a pretty nervy time and our results were a little inconsistent even though for the most part our performances were good and there were a few results that could and should have gone differently. Local derbies against the blue and white shower, where they made little or no attempt to come forward and celebrated a 0-0 draw like they had won the FA Cup, and Rotherham where they bullied us throughout of the game and got a late equaliser after 'Marvellous Marvin Johnson' had cheaply given away the ball when all we needed to do was keep possession resulted in just two points when it should have been six. Then a rare mistake from crowd favourite keeper Henderson, after a dodgy back pass, gave Leeds a win when a point was the least we deserved. We also lost a game to West Brom from a winning position and drew away at a very poor Ipswich Town when a win should have been a given. We had dropped to our lowest position since the end of August and found ourselves in sixth place. (That statement in itself indicates the remarkable progress we have made under Wilder)

Just as good runs come to an end so do bad ones and the Christmas period was one of the best I can remember with four wins on the trot lifting us back into second place. I missed the Derby and Blackburn games due to being away in the Caribbean but our Steve was grateful for the use of the season tickets and reported that the atmosphere at both games was brilliant.

Less than brilliant was the news that while I was searching for the Boxing Day score on the internet I received a phone call telling me that after a seven year long battle with Alzheimer's my mother had passed away on Christmas Day and so the results over Derby and Blackburn were an insignificance for me personally.

The January window was one where everyone was telling us we needed another striker. McGoldrick and Sharp had been producing the goods so far but there was little else to back up that pairing. With Leon Clarke failing to find the previous seasons form and Ben Woodburn failing miserably to fit in with the Blades

175

style, any injury or loss of form from either Sharp or McGoldrick could be costly.

There were however a few loose ends to tie up and, along with making Oliver Norwood's transfer permanent, Wilder also oversaw the permanent departures of Ryan Leonard and Lee Evans. In a surprise move, to me at least, Daniel Lafferty was loaned out and with Keane Bryan not threatening to make the first team squad that left only Marvin Johnson as cover for the wide left positions (scary).

Loans coming in saw our striker issue addressed by bringing in Gary Madine from Cardiff. This was a brave move by Wilder as Madine had long been an enemy of the Blades fans after playing for our city rivals and being particularly obnoxious in the process. He had also had a well-publicised spat with Billy Sharp that was apparently taken much harder by the fans than by Billy himself. Wilder however saw Madine as a viable option and brought him in anyway. To be fair to Madine he was very gracious in the way he acted during his first days at the club and was soon taken to by the Blades fans, who with their usual wit, came up with an appropriate song. **'We've got Madine, Gary Madine, I just don't think you understand: He used to be a twat, he called Billy fat, now he's our scoring machine.'** Brilliant.

Right at the end of the transfer window there was another surprise when Wilder agreed the loan of another long term target in Scott Hogan and at the same time saw Leon Clarke loaned to Wigan. I'm not sure if we came out best in that move as we knew what Leon gave us but had no idea if and when Hogan would ever find his scoring boots. We did however now have twelve million pounds worth of attacking talent on the bench. Not bad by United's standards.

That run of four straight wins over Christmas should have been extended to five wins, but missed chances in a dominant first half at Swansea cost us as they struck half way through the second half to win 1-0. This though gave us the kick up the arse that we needed. A spirited performance at leaders Norwich saw us come from behind twice with Billy Sharp getting both goals in a 2-2 draw. Then back at home, after a nervous first half against a struggling Bolton side, goals from Sharp and McGoldrick gave us a 2-0 victory. It was now shaping up into a three horse race for promotion with Norwich and Leeds just ahead of us and we needed to keep getting the results if we wanted to avoid having to suffer the torture that is the play-offs.

Our next game was a tricky away fixture at Aston Villa and yet again we had been chosen for live TV coverage. Our popularity was good in that, as away tickets were hard to come by, I could still get to see away games live, but I feel we sometimes save our most disappointing performances for the cameras and tend to slip up when most eyes are watching. This may be just something in my head, a false perception, as I know we have also had some of our better moments on live TV and I have not done any research to try and confirm or deny my feelings, it is just one of those niggles that scratch away inside a football fans head. Whatever the truth is this game was one that fed the fire. The game was played on a Friday night and a win would put us top of the league and put pressure on Leeds and Norwich over the weekend. Everything was great for most of the game and the Blades had given Villa a lesson in how to play football once again. We were 3-0 up thanks to a Billy Sharp hat trick and although the cameras showed that we were lucky to have been given one of the goals as Sharp raised his foot to knock the ball away from the keepers hands as he scrambled to grab it, the goal, Billy's one hundredth for the Blades, stood and we were cruising.

I am not sure if Wilder had his eye on the next game but later in the second half he took off Kieron Dowell, who had probably had his best game for the Blades, and that seemed to change the course of the game. From being in total control and looking to increase the score we were now sat back and inviting pressure from Villa. Still with the clock saying eighty two minutes played and with a 3-0 advantage it would be hard to mess it up, wouldn't it?

Villa pressure led to a corner and Dean Henderson made an uncharacteristic mistake and as he flapped at the ball Mings got one back for Villa. The Blades seemed to panic and it was all Villa now and four minutes later a pretty poor shot from the edge of the box was parried away by Henderson when it seemed he could have easily gathered it and Tammy Abraham tapped in to make it 3-2 with four minutes to go. With Sharp now off the pitch, having been substituted, and Washington running about like a headless chicken, we seemed to have no focal point and struggled to keep possession.

Villa just streamed forward in search of an unlikely equaliser and they were unfortunate not to get a penalty when Basham clearly pulled Mings shirt as he tried to get on the end of a corner. Villa could now smell the fear in the Blades defence and with four of the five minutes added time gone the normally reliable Jack O'Connell made what can only be described as a right bollocks of an attempt to clear the ball and Villa pounced to equalise. We had gone from 3-0 up with eight minutes to go and conceded three goals for only the second time in the season and in the end were lucky to have come away with a point.

That result could have been the one that signalled the beginning of the end for the Blades and in previous seasons I am sure it would have. This though was a bunch of spirited players marshalled by a manager that does not know what defeat is and rather than be negatively affected by the eight minute collapse the Blades went on to win six and draw one of the next seven games without conceding a goal. One of those wins was a 1-0 victory at fourth placed West Brom which effectively ended their slim chances of catching up with the top three. The draw was at Hillsborough where their fans once again celebrated what they saw as another 0-0 win.

The last of those seven games without conceding was away to Leeds and while not one of our best performances from an attacking point of view we battled and defended well and when Basham, in a midfield role rather than the more familiar central defensive job, was presented with his second clear run on goal he made no mistake and slotted the ball past the keeper for the only goal of the game and put us into the automatic promotion places with just six games to go.

It now looked like it was down to us or Leeds to accompany Norwich into the Premier League and every point was going to be vital. Our first chance to consolidate our second position came in a home game against Bristol City who were in good form and challenging for a play-off position. The game couldn't have got off to a better start when Billy Sharp headed in from a Fleck free kick on six minutes. All we had to do now was keep another clean sheet. Bristol looked sharp though and after Mcgoldrick had forced a good save from their keeper they came at us. The ball was played down the channel and the usually reliable Enda Stevens made a mess of a simple chance to clear, similar to O'Connell's error at Villa and Bristol scored from the resulting cross to make it 1-1 on the half hour. In the second half City gave us a scare when they hit the post but on seventy one minutes a Baldock cross was met by Scott Hogan to give him his first goal for the club and the Blades a precious 2-1 lead.

The Blades suffered a blow when the man with the magic hat had to go off injured and I was once again left puzzled by Chris Wilder's substitution. Don't get me wrong I am one of Wilders biggest fans and have only ever played and managed a football team at pub league level,so what do I know, but I have often found myself scratching my head at the thought behind some of his substitutions. This time, with a 2-1 lead, a centre half picking up an injury and having two centre halves on the bench, he decided to bring on the waste of space that is Marvin Johnson and slip wing-back Enda Stevens into O'Connell's slot. The result is now a matter of history as Bristol came back from 2-1 down and scored two goals where Johnson could have cleared the danger but instead put in less effort to clear the threat than our lass would have done. Interestingly he has not made the bench since.

At the seventy minute point we were 2-1 up and Leeds were 2-1 down but the fortunes of both sides turned as Bristol went on to win 3-2 and Leeds came back to beat Millwall 3-2 and we were out of the automatic promotion spots once more. The number of games left was starting to dwindle and now it was Leeds who were back in the driving seat.

Our next game was away to Preston North End while Leeds were also away to Birmingham. For once an away team had given the Blades a decent allocation of tickets and with nearly six thousand available my loyalty points allowed me to grab two tickets just fifteen minutes before they sold out, so me and our Steve jumped in the car and headed for Lancashire.

A brilliant following of Blades fans watched on as Preston, who were still harbouring play-off ambitions, came at us early on and Henderson had to be alive to stop a couple of chances. The Blades fans were making all the noise and were rewarded on thirty three minutes when McGoldrick pounced on a loose ball and scored the only goal of the game. All eyes were now on Leeds who were behind to a goal from former Blade Che Adams and as the news of their defeat came in the Blades fans left Deepdale to chants of '*Leeds…..Leeds are falling apart again*' as we regained second spot and advantage in the race for automatic promotion.

The day after the Preston game, before I had chance to tell him about it, my dad died unexpectedly and all thoughts of Sheffield United and their promotion hopes were put on hold.

The following midweek saw me looking on with very mixed emotions as Saturdays fixtures were reversed with us at Birmingham and Leeds away to Preston. Yet again we were on Sky TV and I watched on with just a little less enthusiasm than normal as Enda Stevens lashed the ball into the net to give us a 1-0 lead on thirty eight minutes. Just four minutes later though a corner came in and the initial effort was well blocked only for the ball to fall in the only spot where a Birmingham player could have got it and the score was level again and remained so to the end of the game. Leeds then regained second spot when they beat a ten man Preston team 2-0 and we were once again staring at the play-offs.

To the outsider the race for promotion from the Championship must look very exciting, but for us Blades and presumably the fans just up the road at Leeds it was doing our heads in. One minute we were in the driving seat, the next it looked all over and nothing changed as the days went on.

Next up was a home game against Millwall who were fighting for survival and had given Leeds a run for their money two weeks earlier, while Leeds were to face our city rivals at Elland Road in a televised match immediately following our game. The Millwall game was pretty tight with them giving it a good go in their battle to stay out of the relegation places but when Gary Madine scored to put us in front just after half time it looked like job done. Once again however the Blades seemed to back off and it looked like disaster was on the cards when Millwall were awarded a penalty in the eighty seventh minute after John Egan had made a marvellous save on the line. The referee pointed out that only the goalkeeper was allowed to use his hands and showed Egan the red card.

It seemed like Egan had played a blinder and '*taken one for the team*' when Marshal slammed his spot kick against the bar and there was a collective sigh of relief around Bramall Lane. That relief did not last long though and with just seconds left an effort on goal was parried away by Henderson and just like at Birmingham found the only real danger spot when it flew straight to the head of Millwall defender Cooper who headed home for an equaliser, robbing us of two valuable points.

We all flocked home to our TVs to watch our city rivals play at Leeds and it was strange to think that they might be able to help us out. On the one hand a victory for them would do us a huge favour, but on the other hand I always wanted them to lose. Most Blades, certainly of my generation, tend to look at their results even before our own. Years of not so friendly banter exchanged between the two sets of fans means that if they have lost then no matter what our result is we won't be in for an ear bashing the next day. On this occasion however I found myself willing the blue and white side to hang on as a dominant Leeds side battered at their goal. Westwood played a blinder in the first half making three great saves and although they never looked like winning it seemed like the Hillsborough side might hang on. It was not to be though and when Harrison scored the only goal of the game on sixty five minutes my disappointment was tempered by the fact that at least the other lot would not be able to claim they helped us to promotion. We were however now second favourites to go up automatically with just four games left. It would seem that we would need to win them all and hope that Leeds slipped up if we were to claim an automatic promotion spot and avoid a ninth attempt at the play-offs.

A little alcoholic cockney fella once said '*It's a funny old game*' in reference to football and so it turns out. The Easter fixture list had pitted the Blades against Forest in a Good Friday lunchtime kick-off while Leeds played at home to Wigan in the afternoon. These games were to be quickly followed on Easter Monday by a trip to Hull for us and an away match at Brentford for Leeds. This was a critical period in the Championship promotion race and on paper Leeds held the advantage. Wigan were struggling towards the foot of the table and had a terrible away record while Forest were still in with a chance of making a late run for the play-off spots. Even with a win over Forest we were not expecting to make up ground on Leeds and I was nervously glancing at our respective goal differences as it looked like it could come down to that and our advantage was only quite slender.

The Forest game saw the Blades looking a little edgy and nowhere near their best in the first half and there were mumblings on the kop as it looked as though we were not going to catch Leeds this day. The second half though saw an improvement in the Blades play. The Blades went at Forest from the start and when McGoldrick burst towards the box, and a clear chance on goal, a Forest defender had little choice but to chop him down and receive a red card as his reward. The resulting free kick produced nothing but within a couple of minutes, as Forest were still trying to reorganise, Duffy, who had been pretty quiet until then, curled a delightful shot over the Forest keeper from twenty yards and we were ahead.

It was still quite tense as the ten man Forest team tried to shut up shop but the tension was cut when, after some good build up play, Enda Stevens fired home from a tight angle on eighty five minutes to make sure of the points. I headed home and rather than sit and watch news of the Leeds game on Soccer Saturday I did some work in the garden to try and ease the tension. I managed to avoid news from Elland Road until our lass popped her head out of the window and told me that Wigan were winning, but were playing with ten men. I didn't want to get my hopes up so I said *'Leeds will still win, they always do,'* but inside I was willing the little Lancashire club to hang on. At the end of the game my missus hit me with the incredible news that ten man Wigan had indeed hung on to beat Leeds 2-1 and it looked like it was game on again as we leapfrogged Leeds back into second spot.

Next up were Hull and what looked like a tricky game at a ground where we had been very poor at a similar stage of the previous season. It was now twitchy bum time and we knew any slip up could be disastrous. Leeds though were in a similar position and their trip to Brentford, a side that were capable of beating anyone on their day, would not be easy. It was starting to look like a war of nerves.

The Blades who had a team scattered with players who had been in this position before held their nerve fantastically and ended up 3-0 winners with first half goals from McGoldrick (2), the second being a brilliant twenty five yard shot, and Stevens to wrap up a comfortable win. Our attention now turned to London where the Brentford v Leeds game was being played at five fifteen for a Sky TV audience. I along with many other Blades tuned in and became an honorary Brentford fan for a couple of hours.

The nerves were clearly showing in the Leeds players as they went at Brentford, but struggled to find the quality needed in front of goal. The Leeds front foot tactics were made for Brentford who had made a reputation as a good counter attacking team and as Leeds threw players forward Brentford broke and gave Leeds a scare on a few occasions before, almost on the stroke of half time, Maupay sprinted onto a ball slid between the Leeds defenders and produced a classy finish to put the home side ahead.

The second half saw more of the same and, as Leeds seemed to be running out of ideas with the highly rated Jack Clarke on as substitute looking out of his depth, Brentford got a decisive second goal with a clever little finish from the impressive Canos. I was watching the game at home in Barnsley, but I am sure I could hear cheering from Sheffield as the final whistle went.

In a matter of just four days our fortunes had turned around dramatically and our two wins, combined with Leeds two defeats, meant that with just two games left we were three points clear of Leeds and with an eleven goal advantage in goal difference. Our next game is against bottom club Ipswich Town at Bramall lane and any sort of win will put us in a position where we are just about certain of automatic promotion. Surely even a club with a history of biblically proportioned cock ups can't blow it from here, can we?

***

As I sit here and write this I am now fully up to date with the story of my lifetime of following Sheffield United. My next sight of the red and white shirts will be on Saturday 27[th]April at Bramall Lane and anything that I write from here on is written in real time.

Just to let you know, my feelings are all over the place. We are poised on the brink of a return to the Premier League for the first time since 2007 but my excitement is also tinged with a little fear. The Premier League has changed beyond recognition since the last time we were there and having watched some of the current teams in action, including the recent Champions League quarter-final between Man City and Spurs, the thought of the Blades facing these sort of teams next season fills me with dread.

After seeing the Blades win regularly for the last eight seasons, am I ready for the potential thrashings that seem to be waiting around the corner? Do I want to see the Blades suffer a similar fate to that of Fulham and Huddersfield this season? Will we be able to do what Wolves have done this season, or will we go the way of so many teams over the last few years and see a quick return to the Championship?

I am getting ahead of myself though. We are not there yet and anything but a win on Saturday could still see us blow it at the last minute yet again and condemn us to the dreaded play-offs once more. Just because Ipswich are bottom of the table and already relegated does not mean that we are guaranteed a win. Our biggest enemy could yet be ourselves and, if there is any complacency among our players, Ipswich could still be capable of springing a surprise. The natural pessimism is still trying to break through even at this stage; that is what watching the Blades in six different decades has done to me. We have had our share of promotions over the years, but as we stand here on the brink of what could be the biggest one yet it is still the last gasp relegations and glorious failures that nag away at the back of my mind. But do you know what, I am not going to let the negative thoughts win........Fuck it; bring on the Tractor boys.

It was raining as we arrived at the ground and I tried recall if any of our previous promotions had been gained in the rain. I couldn't think of any, the big ones at Darlington and Leicester were definitely in full sunshine Recently at Northampton it was sunny again. Way back in 1971 when we played Watford off the pitch the sun was shining. I can't remember a drop of rain on any of the occasions where we had been promoted, but then again on all of those occasions the last thing on my mind was the weather. Was todays wind and rain a bad omen or would a full blown hurricane not be able to stop us this time.

It was good to see a few Ipswich fans had made the journey up from Suffolk and the Blades fans were mingling with some of them who were in fancy dress and good spirits despite their side having already been relegated. Our fans could relate to their predicament having been there before on a number of occasions.

A lot of the pubs around the ground had been put on restricted entry and that was probably the reason that the ground started to fill earlier than usual for the five fifteen kick off and the beer and pies were selling faster than they had been for the other home games this season. I was with my mates Paul, the one who had got me the tickets at Burton the previous season, and Ralph who had been coming along since his wife had bought him a mini season ticket next to me as a surprise at Christmas. Our Steve was working and although he really wanted to be there it looked like his four on, four off shift pattern was going to prevent him joining the party.

As the minutes ticked away towards kick off and the crowd started to find its voice, a little louder and earlier than usual, it was clear that the atmosphere was going to be something special, even by Bramall Lane standards. I was looking around trying to take it all in when I was grabbed from behind and had someone shouting '*We are Blades, We are Blades*' in my ear. I turned around to see our Steve stood behind me with a huge grin on his face. He had got off work early and made sure he was not going to miss what should be a special day in the Blades history and I was glad to have him there beside me.

The team came out to a magnificent reception and the kop was starting to bounce. The Greasy Chip Butty song was sung as loud as I have ever heard it as the Blades set about their task, taking the game to Ipswich from the kick off. The team had just one change from the starting line-up at Hull the previous Monday with *Henderson, Baldock, Stevens, Basham, Egan, O'Connell, Norwood, Fleck, Duffy, McGoldrick and Hogan* starting the game. *Cranie* had dropped to the bench to make way for Basham and club captain *Billy Sharp* had regained enough fitness, after a hamstring injury, to also take a place on the subs bench beside *Madine, Lundstam, Dowell, Stearman* and *Moore*.

Early pressure on Ipswich saw a couple of chances go begging as McGoldrick and Hogan missed opportunities. The Ipswich fans must have been rueing their clubs decision to let McGoldrick go for free in a season where he looked like being promoted to the

Premier League as his former team mates were heading for League One.

After squandering those early chances the Blades had to be on their guard as a spirited Ipswich side defied their league position and tried to mount a few attacks of their own. As the minutes ticked by the crowd in the ground continued to give good vocal backing, but I could sense a little tension creeping in as the score remained goalless. Then on twenty four minutes, after a couple of fruitless raids forward, centre back Jack O'Connell again popped up in the overlapping role that had perplexed so many opposition sides in the last three years and delivered a hard, low cross into the six yard box which was met near the front post by Scott Hogan and as the net at the Bramall Lane end bulged the crowd went wild as the dream of the Premier League came a step closer.

The party was now in full swing and, as the minutes ticked by and all the usual songs were belted out, efforts from Norwood and Baldock came close to increasing our lead. A little spice was added to the mix when Ipswich midfielder Judge went in late on O'Connell and received a booking as the referee tried to stop the situation escalating into a scuffle. The half time whistle blew and I got a chance to sit down for a few minutes with the Blades just forty five minutes from the top flight.

The second half started just as the first had ended with Ipswich valiantly trying to make a game of it but never really threatening Henderson's goal and the Blades pressing for the second goal that would give us the breathing space we needed on such a high pressure day. Norwood hit the post from a free kick and then a McGoldrick header at the far post went agonisingly close with half the thirty thousand crowd thinking the ball had gone in the net.

Just after the hour mark Wilder brought off goal scorer Hogan and replaced him with Blades talisman Billy Sharp and his reception got a cheer almost as loud as the one that had greeted the goal. *'Billy Sharp, Billy Sharp, We've got Billy Sharp'* rang around the ground as the lifelong Blades fan took to the pitch, soon to be followed by choruses of the promotion themed song *'Jack O'Connell's Magic'* as the minutes ticked closer to the end.

A Norwood corner was met by an unmarked John Egan and his header flew inches over the bar as the Blades pressed for that vital second goal. That goal was not long coming as from the very next corner, delivered by Fleck, the man with the magic hat powered in a headed to make it 2-0 on seventy one minutes.

The crowd were now ecstatic and all the old and new chants rang out around the ground. Six minutes later all four sides of the ground, including the entire Ipswich following, rose and applauded David McGoldrick as Wilder replaced him with Gary Madine, giving the former Ipswich striker the chance to receive a thoroughly deserved standing ovation. Next to receive the crowds applause was the ever willing Mark Duffy who was replaced by John Lundstram for the last few minutes.

The game was almost over and the celebrations had already started when Henderson tipped over the first Ipswich shot on target and as the last seconds of the two minutes added time ticked by the referees final whistle could not be heard above the noise and so our celebrations were kicked off with the sight of the players all throwing their hands in the air as the official ended the game.

The plan had been for the players to leave the field and then return to do a lap around the ground to express their appreciation to the fans, but wild horses could not have dragged any of them off and, after they had gathered together to celebrate amongst themselves, they paraded around the ground to take the applause from the thirty thousand fans, including most of the Ipswich followers who had stayed behind and graciously joined in with the applause, particularly for their ex-striker McGoldrick who took the time to break off from the rest of the players and return their gesture. As the players finally headed towards the tunnel the Blades fans gave one more chorus of the Greasy Chip Butty song and slowly headed off to celebrate what was effectively, if not quite mathematically certain, promotion to the Premier League.

Despite the wind and rain and despite the fact that there was still a mathematical, if not realistic, possibility that Leeds could still catch us I spent the night popping the champagne corks and opening the bar in my back garden as I celebrated our promotion with friends and family. I raised a glass in a toast to my dad who, despite having not been to see the Blades play for many a year, had been the one who introduced me to the Blades and always asked me how they had gone on every time I visited him. I just hope that wherever he is now the news of our promotion gets through.

On Sunday morning I woke early with a surprisingly clear head and pottered about until it was time to watch Leeds v Villa in a game that could see that mathematical issue resolved.

Sheffield United have been involved in some dramatic end of season situations, but what I have just witnessed is right up there on the top of the pile. In a game that was well contested for a long time there was the most incredible and bizarre turn of events.

During the game a Leeds player was down injured and Villa, despite being in a good attacking position, sportingly put the ball out of play so that treatment could be given to the Leeds man. Later in the game with the score still 0-0 Villa forward Kodjia was caught by a Leeds defender and was laid, clearly in pain, in the Leeds half. Leeds had the ball by the half way line and the Villa players were signalling to the Leeds man to put the ball out of play. Instead, as the Villa players stopped and waited for the ball to be played out, Tyler Roberts, the Leeds man played the ball up the line to Klich who went on to score. There was than a lot of pushing and shoving in an incident in which a Villa player was given a red card after Patrick Bamford went down clutching his face as the Villa man appeared to swing an arm at him, but the replay showed there was no contact.

I have to give full credit here to a magnificent gesture from Leeds manager Marcelo Bielsa as he instructed his bunch of despicable, unsporting players to allow Villa to go up the field from the kick off and score an equalising goal, despite, centre back Jansson attempting to defy his managers orders and try to stop Adomah putting the ball into the net.

The scores were back level and, despite some intense pressure from Leeds, ten man Villa managed to hang on for the draw that meant the Blades were now officially promoted to the Premier League.

Just like in 2006 the final whistle of a 1-1 draw at Elland Road signalled the exact moment of our promotion. It is unlikely, but I would love the records to show the Villa goal that confirmed our promotion to read '*Scorer – Albert Adomah, Assist – Marcelo Bielsa.,*' Seemingly the only honourable man at the Leeds club.

WE ARE PREMIER LEAGUE, WE ARE PREMIER LEAGUE.

188

The final game of the season at Stoke City was sold out to Blades fans in no time at all and so I was facing the prospect of watching scores come through on the TV as the Blades looked for the win and hoped that Villa could beat Norwich City in a combination of results that could see us crowned champions. But, good news came through as the Football League approved plans to beam-back coverage of the final game of the season to Bramall Lane so, while I can't be at the Bet 365 Stadium, at least I will be able to watch the game live. The last time I watched a beam back was when we clinched the League One title so, who knows, having the big screens there again might just prove to be a good omen.

I was a little disappointed, but not exactly surprised, when before the game I had a peek at the team that Villa had put out for the final game against Norwich. With Jack Grealish perilously close to a ban after picking up a bagful of yellow cards, probably mostly for diving or dissent, he was left out of the squad altogether and El Mohamady and El-Ghazi, who had both impressed at Leeds the previous week, were dropped to the bench. It was clear that Villa had now got their eyes on the play-off games and I can't blame them for that. They have their own best interests to think of and helping us to win the title was not their priority. We however still had to do our bit and hope for the best elsewhere.

The atmosphere for the beam-back was again a little strange as the fans in the John Street stand faced the three big screens on the edge of the pitch with the emptiness of the other three sides of the ground as a backdrop. As the match got underway it was the Blades who were on top early on but the tempo of the game was not high and with us still having an outside chance of winning the title I was a little surprised that we were not a little snappier in the tackle and quicker going forward.

It did not take long for news to filter through that Norwich had taken the lead at Villa Park but within a few minutes Villa got one back and we still had a chance of the title. Stoke, against the run of play, then went one up after a poor attempt at a clearing header fell to Vokes who smashed his shot past Henderson. Not exactly what we wanted, but the Blades responded and pressed for an equaliser. It should have been level before half time but a shot from Billy was handled by Shawcross on the line and deflected onto the post with the officials missing the infringement.

189

At half time Wilder took off Duffy and Norwood and gave some game time to Dowell and Lundstram. It was soon looking like a bit of tactical genius when three minutes into the second half Dowell got on the end of a Fleck pass and rifled the ball home to make it 1-1. The Blades were looking better in the second half but Stoke were still getting a bit of joy on the counter-attack and, with the tempo still not as high as I would have liked from a Blades side still clinging on to a chance of winning the title, the game was looking like it was going to end in stalemate. Then from a Stoke corner there was an almighty lapse in concentration and Shawcross couldn't believe his luck as he wandered into the six yard box unmarked to tap home a second for Stoke.

The Blades were not going to let it go though and started to play more like the side that had won promotion to the Premier League and after a couple of flowing moves had come close another good attack saw the ball played by Sharp into the path of Stevens who made no mistake in banging the ball past Stoke keeper Butland to level the scores again. The atmosphere in the seats in the John Street stand picked up a bit, but it was nothing compared to the atmosphere on the concourse underneath where more and more fans were starting to gather and watch the game on the many TV sets around the bar area. It was bouncing down there and the promotion party was in full swing.

The Blades pressed for a winner, but it was not to be and as the time ticked away the news came through that Norwich had done what they had been doing all season and had snatched a late winner making our result insignificant. As the final whistle went the celebrations really kicked off at Stoke with the entire Blades following staying inside the Bet 365 stadium to join in with the team's celebrations on the pitch in front of them as the players came forward from the group one by one to take the applause and dance to their own songs.

The slim chances of the title had gone, and I must give my congratulations here to Norwich who just kept notching up the results while all eyes seemed to be on the battle between us and Leeds for the second spot. Well done to Daniel Farke and his team for a great achievement. See you next season.

The final table showed that we had been promoted in second place, five points behind Champions Norwich City and six points ahead of third placed Leeds United. The title would have been the icing on the cake but, considering the resources that Chris Wilder had available to him, second place and that all important place in the Premier League next season is still a truly remarkable achievement and it seems incredible that less than three years ago we were sat at the bottom of League one. What a journey and what a manager.

It could have been very difficult to come up with the words to describe what Chris Wilder has managed to achieve for the Blades but fortunately the masses on the kop have come up with those words for me.

'It was our sixth year in Division One,
When Chris Wilder came home,
He took us to the very top,
He's one of our own,
HE'S ONE OF OUR OWN.'

What Happens Next?

So there we are, back in the top flight of English football. Forty eight years after I stood on the kop with my dad and watched Tony Currie and his team mates gain promotion to the First Division, I stood on that very same end of the ground beside my (somewhat older) son and watched Chris Wilder's group of players do the same thing as they reached the dizzy heights, and the pot of gold, that is the Premier League.

In between there has been a journey that has seen eight relegations, eight promotions, eight unsuccessful play-off competitions, six cup semi-finals, patches of brilliance and periods of mediocrity. There has been drama and controversy, joy and despair. I have seen the sublime and the ridiculous; I have seen promotions won by the narrowest of margins and relegations sealed by virtually the last kick of the game.

Following the Blades over six different decades, I have seen the fans who have stuck with them put through a roller coaster of emotions and it is because of that, not in spite of it, that it has been so good. As I wrote at the very beginning of this book it is the lows that make the highs so special. It is the controversial defeats and the glorious failures that make the promotions and titles won so much better. It is the fact that we are still seen as an unfashionable club, punching above our weight, that makes us so proud to stand up and declare that '*We are Blades, We are Blades, O we are, we are Blades*'

So what happens next? What does the future hold in store? Our next season will be played in the toughest league in the world. The club will be rewarded with millions of pounds worth of TV and advertising money. History indicates that only a small proportion of that money will end up invested in the team and I am fine with that. After a season that has seen Fulham invest all their Premier League riches in trying to build a side that can stay in the top flight, yet still be relegated by Easter, I would not want to see the Blades go the same way and waste those rewards. Yes we need some new players if we are to cope in the top flight, but we need players with the right mentality for this club, not fly by night, money grabbing, journeymen whose heads will drop at the first sign of a struggle.

The odds are that, whoever stays and whoever comes in, our return to the top will be a long hard battle for survival and we may not win that battle. That is ok; the important thing is that we stay in shape for the next battle and the one after that. Other clubs have hit the top and struggled after a quick relegation, Sunderland are one of the latest examples, suffering back to back relegations. Not all that long ago a little man called Jimmy Sirrel took Notts County, a founder member of the Football League, to the top flight. In this same season that we regained our Premier League status they lost their battle against relegation to non-league football. Bolton Wanderers, not too long ago a team to be reckoned with in the top flight under Sam Allardyce, this season faced bankruptcy and saw wages unpaid and failed to put out a team towards the end of the season.

There is a saying *'Be careful what you wish for.'* Well we have wished for a return to the top and that wish has been granted. What we now need is for the infighting in the boardroom to be settled and for the club's owners to sensibly manage the future to ensure that the Blades; our Blades; continue to prosper and do not fall into the same traps as they have before.

I am pretty sure that we are not going to emulate Manchester City; we will never be a new Manchester United. The billions that have been invested in Chelsea will never come our way and I for one am not bothered. We are a club of the fans, a club of the people of Sheffield and I hope that we can remain so. I would not want to see a little success bringing in the sheiks or oligarchs and turning our unique club into a billionaire's plaything, where winning a European trophy and finishing second in the league is seen as failure and results in the sacking of the manager. As Chris Wilder said in an emotional and possibly lager fuelled interview immediately after our promotion was confirmed. The owners of this club are simply custodians; the club belongs to the fans.

Our target now is not to compete with Spurs and Arsenal but to try and emulate the likes of Southampton and Bournemouth, Watford and Brighton and retain our place at the top table so that we can build slowly and solidly over a sustained period. If we have to go down and back up again to build that base, as Burnley have done, then so be it. What we must avoid is going the way of Blackpool or Barnsley, Swindon or Luton where a brief spell at the top is followed by years of decline and struggle. Where else have we seen that before? We must learn from the mistakes of the past.

We have an opportunity to grow and establish this wonderful club and who knows if we can get the basics right and manage the club through what could be a difficult first season then one season somewhere down the line this small unfashionable club of the people might just be able to achieve what a similar small unfashionable club seventy miles south of here did in 2016.

We have in our manager a man that represents what this club is all about. We have a similar man in our club captain. We have an academy that in the past has produced players that have gone on to play in the Premier League and for their country. It is my hope that someday fairly soon we can produce, and hang onto, more players like Kyle Walker, Harry Maguire, Phil Jagielka, Dominic Calvert-Lewin, Matthew Lowton and David Brooks who are all currently playing in the Premier League.

I do not know if Chris Wilder will go on to be the greatest manager Sheffield United has ever had. He is certainly getting close, but he has only had three years in charge. Will he find the Premier League, with its big budgets, big headed foreign players and tactically wise, internationally proven managers a step too far as Neil Warnock seems to have done with us, QPR and Cardiff? Or will he thrive and grow? And if he does will we be able to hang onto him?

One thing I am pretty sure of is that Wilder will not be around forever. Relegation next season is not inevitable, but nor would it be a surprise and if that is the fate that awaits us the board must be strong and stick with the man who is best placed to lead us back up again. (If relegation does come our way, please keep Sean Bean away from the manager.) The ownership battle may go the way of the man from Saudi Arabia and like many other new foreign owners he may be tempted to bring in a *'Big name'* as his own man. Wilder himself strikes me as a man who, while he loves this club, will not stand for any bullshit or lack of ambition on the part of the board and it may be he that walks away rather than be given the same sort of treatment that Nigel Spackman received.

Players come and go, chairmen and managers come and go, but the one constant is the fans. All I ask of whoever is out there representing this great club is that they remember that and look after it on our behalf so that when I, and everyone else of my generation, are long gone and forgotten there is still a team in Sheffield that can;

'Fill up my senses, like a gallon of Magnet,
Like a packet of Woodbines,
Like a good pinch of snuff,
Like a night out in Sheffield,
Like a greasy chip butty,
Like Sheffield United,
Come fill me again.
Na Na Na Na Na Na Na Ooohh.

Other books by Alan Allsop

Barmy Army

*Based on actual events back in the days when being a football
hooligan was relatively harmless fun. This story recalls the tale of
a Sheffield United fan and a small group of his friends travelling
the country to watch football matches in the late seventies and
early eighties. Spending days and nights out in unfamiliar towns,
getting into scrapes and getting up to daft tricks. Fighting? Yes
there was plenty of fighting, and many of the scraps are recalled
here, but there was more to it than that. In what aims to be more
than just a catalogue of terrace battles, Alan Allsop gives a
personal insight into the characters, the exploits and the laughs
enjoyed by just one of the many small gangs that came together on
match days to form 'The Barmy Army'*

You Couldn't Make it Up

*When Alan Allsop started work as an Apprentice Plumber back in
1976 he expected working life to be hard, serious and anything but
fun. However, 27 years of working for Sheffield City Council's
Works Department turned out to be just the opposite. In this
amusing recollection of working life, Alan describes the reality of
working for a large bureaucratic organisation from his humble
beginnings as a £19 per week apprentice to becoming a Contract's
Manager overseeing a budget in the millions. The scams, the
antics and the characters he came across as he rose through the
ranks are recalled in detail here in this story. Parts of this tale
may seem strange, crazy, even absurd, but as Alan found out as he
worked his way up, no matter how bizarre some of the situations
he came across may sound.
You just couldn't make it up.*

The Soundtrack of an Ordinary Life

Do you ever hear an old song and are immediately reminded of a time from your past? Of course you do; we all do.

Spurred by his own musical reminders, Alan Allsop tells the story of his life. Childhood innocence; teenage angst; overcoming bullying; dreams achieved; dreams shattered; joy and tragedy, fun and fears. A whole range of emotions over the best part of sixty years are laid out here. The various strands of his life: love, family, career and a lifelong dedication to following Sheffield United are bound together by the underlying humour that helped him through it.

Punctuated by references to around 700 songs that trigger the memories, the ups and downs of life's rollercoaster are detailed here in Alan's own forthright style.

With something for everyone to relate to, and ponder over, Alan tells it how it was for him.

An ordinary life?...........You decide.

Twisted Psyche

Not for the faint hearted or overly sensitive and with more than the occasional expletive, Alan Allsop pulls together a collection of poems written over a period of more than thirty years as the school of hard knocks taught him that life is not always easy.

Do not expect poems in the style of Wordsworth, Shelly or Byron. Alan writes in the same down to earth, often hard hitting style with which he has lived his life.

With no punches pulled and often driven by a range of strong emotions, Alan exposes his tormented inner psyche as life tried and failed to knock him down.

While some of the pieces are dark, even when he was writing the darkest of pieces he was usually smiling, if somewhat sardonically, inside. That's the way he is, that's what keeps him going and that underlying humour occasionally peeps through.

Printed in Great Britain
by Amazon

33901989R00113